THE TRANSFORMATION SERIES
Gay Hendricks, *General Editor*

Books in The Transformation Series
explore the transitions of human life
and the possibilities
for happier, more creative living through the application
of the psychology of adjustment.

Books in the series:

How to Love Every Minute of Your Life
by Gay Hendricks and Carol Leavenworth

The Family Centering Book:
Awareness Activities the Whole Family Can Do Together
by Gay Hendricks

Act Yourself:
Stop Playing Roles and Unmask Your True Feelings
by Jo Loudin

Talk to Yourself: Using the Power of Self-Talk
by Charles Zastrow

Divorce: How and When to Let Go
by Nancy Williamson Adam and John H. Adam

You're Divorced, But Your Children Aren't
by T. Roger Duncan and Darlene Duncan

I Know What's Wrong, But I Don't Know What to Do About It
by Arnold P. Goldstein, Robert P. Sprafkin, and N. Jane Gershaw

Gay Hendricks is an associate professor of counseling at the University of Colorado at Colorado Springs and a psychologist in private practice. His doctorate, in counseling psychology, is from Stanford University. Among his other books are *The Centering Book, The Second Centering Book, Transpersonal Education,* and *How to Love Every Minute of Your Life.* He and his family live in Colorado Springs.

gay hendricks

the family centering book

awareness
activities
the whole family
can do
together

A SPECTRUM BOOK

Prentice-Hall, Inc.
Englewood Cliffs, New Jersey 07632

Library of Congress Cataloging in Publication Data

Hendricks, Gay.
  The family centering book.

  (The Transformation series) (A Spectrum Book)
  Includes index.
  1. Family.   2. Problem solving, Group.   3. Self-
actualization (Psychology)—Problems, exercises, etc.
I. Title.

HQ734.H477   301.42   79-12580
ISBN 0-13-301846-6
ISBN 0-13-301838-5 pbk.

*For my mother, Norma Canaday Hendricks.
And for the family of all of us.*

A Spectrum Book

10 9 8 7 6 5 4 3 2 1

Editorial/production supervision
and interior design by Eric Newman
Manufacturing buyer: Cathie Lenard

Prentice-Hall International, Inc., *London*
Prentice-Hall of Australia Pty. Limited, *Sydney*
Prentice-Hall of Canada, Ltd., *Toronto*
Prentice-Hall of India Private Limited, *New Delhi*
Prentice-Hall of Japan, Inc., *Tokyo*
Prentice-Hall of Southeast Asia Pte. Ltd., *Singapore*
Whitehall Books Limited, *Wellington, New Zealand*

contents

how to solve problems and build responsibility

meditation, relaxation, and centering activities for the whole family

family dreamwork

discussions

Child Developmental Stages
and What to Do About Them

How to Give Permissions
without Being Permissive

acknowledgments

I am deeply grateful to the many persons who have helped me develop a sense of family. These are people who through deep love, and sometimes deep adversity, helped me find the space to be who I am. My mother, to whom this book is dedicated, is a remarkable and talented person. Michael Hendricks, my brother, was an anchor to me as I grew up. I am grateful also to my formidable grandparents Elmer and Rebecca Delle Canaday, both of whom loved me in their own ways. The kindness of my aunts, Audrey Canaday Williamson, Lynndelle Canaday Hoover, and Catherine Canaday, is remembered with gratitude and, at the moment I write this, tears. My father, who died just before I was born, left me a legacy I shall perhaps never be able to describe. I am thankful to my daughter, Amanda Delle Hendricks, for her gifts of love, honesty, and incredible charm. Susie and Steve have taught me a great deal about loving and communicating in families. I owe much to my wife, Carol Leavenworth, not only for her love and wit, but also because meeting her was one of my life's great experiences. All of these family members, and more, have held my hand as I journeyed forward to discover the magnificent surprise that I am a member of a large family indeed: the one in which we all abide and that abides in all of us.

introduction:
a sense
of family

We humans like to experience a sense of family, and there are good reasons for this yearning. After all, a human being is a family of cells. What is humankind itself but a large family contributing to the larger family of the universe? Arrange for a small family of oxygen and hydrogen to come together and you have water. So, up and down the scale, we yearn to form families, groups of beings uniting to enhance the well-being of all.

One of the most satisfying things that human beings do is to develop bonds within families. There is something indefinably good about relating closely with our kin. It's clear to everyone, though, that the good feelings in families are hard to come by and hard to maintain. No sooner do we feel comfortable and on top of things than the good feelings slip away again, elusive as a butterfly's shadow. This is doubly frustrating to us these days because the present is a time of tremendous psychological and spiritual growth. Many people feel that they are rapidly liberating themselves from old, limiting patterns and moving toward greater happiness and satisfaction. Yet often it is difficult to share our growth and change with our families. It would be very satisfying to be able to have our psychological and spiritual growth along with increased harmony and relatedness with our families, both the families we grew up in and the ones we live in now.

It is possible to develop a sense of family centeredness, that relaxed sense of harmony that means we are experiencing a greater unity with ourselves and others. That is what this book is about. First, though, we need to acknowledge the barriers that must be dissolved in order to experience centeredness in the family.

Let us begin by accepting that it is not possible to always have pleasant things happen in the family. Sometimes we have the sense that when things go wrong, it is a catastrophe. Let's accept at the beginning that sometimes things will hum and feel good, and sometimes they will rattle and bump and feel bad. That's the way it is. Part of growing a centered family is to accept that you will gain that sense of centeredness and then promptly lose it. Then you will gain it again and lose it again. Being centered is losing being centered as well as getting it back again. At a workshop in which I was sharing this point of view, a man shouted, "Whoopee! That takes the pain out of losing it!" Exactly. One of the things we need to do is to quit being hard on ourselves for making mistakes. If we tie our good feelings to *achieving* things (like being centered), we then have to feel bad when we lose it, which we will inevitably do. So, an alternative is to feel good about both getting that sense of centeredness and losing it. The magic in this awareness is that at the moment you feel okay about not feeling centered, you get centered again.

We also need to accept ourselves for being inept at dealing with our close relationships. To begin with, few of us have any training in how to relate. Many of us grew up in families in which the interaction patterns were anything but healthy. This means that we bring to our present lives a history of negative learning coupled with little training in how to relate in a positive way. We need, therefore, to give ourselves much permission to be novices at one of the most difficult jobs of all: relating to our close ones from a centered place.

In our lives, we also need to acknowledge that many of our feelings, thoughts, and behaviors are influenced by the family in which we grew up. How close we get, how we express feelings, how we solve problems, and other key issues are all programmed by how we saw those things happen around us when we were growing up. Part of growing a centered family is observing patterns from our old families being acted out in our present lives and dissolving those old patterns so that we can live in the present.

Our beliefs and expectations about what family life ought to be like are one of the major inheritances from our original families. We often get so stuck in the beliefs that are handed down to us that we cannot tell where belief ends and reality begins. Spotting and dissolving the shoulds, oughts, don'ts, and other inhibiting beliefs we carry around from the past can be one of the most liberating things we can do. To enhance our personal evolution, as well as our growth within the family, we need to keep asking ourselves the question "How is my present life being influenced by what I experienced in my family as I was growing up?" The answers can be profoundly disturbing. They will always be profoundly interesting.

Another barrier that blocks our centeredness in the family is our amateur status in knowing how to handle feelings. Dealing with feelings, our own and those of others around us, is one of life's major skills, and as is common with central life skills, we are given almost no training in how to do it. The closer we are to one another, the deeper are the feelings that are called up. In families, the deeper feelings of anger, hurt, fear, and joy happen all the time, even though these feelings may be deeply repressed, so family life is one of our major opportunities to find out what feelings are all about and how to deal with them. If we can use this opportunity, rather than fight it, the rewards are enormous.

A barrier that many families find difficult to transcend is the inability to make and keep meaningful agreements. The family is a place where people can learn important life skills about how to handle agreements. Real responsibility can be taught in the family. The difference between real responsibility and what often passes for responsibility is an important one. False responsibility has to do with fear and guilt. We act "responsibly" because we have been threatened with punishment. Real responsibility means the ability to evaluate our own behavior to see how it can bring about positive consequences for us and others. Learning to make agreements that are satisfying to everyone and learning to keep those agreements can be a major source of centeredness in the family.

Families are also places where problems frequently occur, and where there is much need for clear communication. Our dearth of good problem-solving strategies and our lack of information in how to go about communicating clearly with one another present a formidable barrier that must be overcome if we are to experience centeredness in the family. When families can evolve good problem-solving strategies and open up channels of clear communication, much harmony can be experienced.

The last barrier we will observe is that although families often *do* a lot of things together, few families are able to find ways of *being* together. *Being* in this context refers to those moments in which we experience the expansion of self, those times when we get beyond our roles and increase our ability to know ourselves and feel in greater harmony with ourselves and others. We all hope, of course, that families will set the stage for these moments to occur spontaneously. Sometimes the growth of being does occur, but more often our experience is that we get lost in *doing* to the negelct of our *being*. The centered family is one in which there are many opportunities to *be* together.

In this book, I will describe many ways of dissolving each of these barriers. Our task will be to find out how we can grow a centered family in such a way that individuals within the family unit will have a set of skills that, with time and loving practice, can bring them to full unity with themselves, with others, and with the universe.

To grow a lovely garden, you need good seeds, good tools, and careful, loving attention. You also must not be afraid to get down on your hands and knees and get your hands dirty. If we can bring the same qualities of love, attention, and bravery to bear on working with our families, a rich and bountiful harvest will be ours. I propose that we begin by finding out more about what families are for. Then we can explore how to deal with feelings and how to talk to one another. With a firm foundation of clear communication, we can find out how to solve problems effectively. We will develop several specific problem-solving strategies, and then we will turn our attention to finding ways of being together through meditation, movement, relaxation, dreams, and other activities.

what
families
are about

Families are all about learning, and learning is perhaps the best thing humans do. When we really stop and think about it, there are few things more satisfying than learning important skills, knowledge, and sensitivities. Families are the best place of all to learn the most important things humans need to learn.

Earlier in evolution, it was crucial for humans to learn to use tools. So, families were places where we learned about rock-chipping, corn-grinding, and, much later, skills like sawing, hammering, and butter-churning. Now, especially in technological societies like those in America and Europe, where the tools are very sophisticated, the focus has shifted: We are now learning to use *ourselves.* In a world that depends on good human relationships, families are places where we can learn to use ourselves well. We can learn to be aware of our own feelings and needs, and we can learn to be sensitive to the needs and feelings of others. So this is an era of evolution in which we most need to learn good human relations— how to be at home with ourselves and with other people.

FAMILIES ARE MAGIC MIRRORS

The reason families are the best place to learn good human relations is that family life is a mirror—one of the kind that magnifies everything. In families, the magnifying mirror lets us see what we need to learn. If lets us look (often painfully) at what works and what doesn't. It lets us see the very worst in ourselves and others, and the very best.

One thing that can help make our family lives smoother is realizing that we don't have to do it right. First of all, there's no right way to be an effective parent or child. Remember that we are all in a process of learning to do this most important of all things—be at home with ourselves and others—with almost no training. Too, the process of learning involves doing lots of things that don't work. We need to learn to feel okay about doing things that don't work because if we don't, we are going to feel bad a lot of the time. Looking at the example of Leonardo da Vinci helped me realize this. Reading his notebooks, it is easy to see that he was one of the most creative people of all time, yet we see in his notes that many of his experiments didn't work. The machine would fall apart, the paint wouldn't go on right (think of how many smiles he must have gone through before he got Mona Lisa's right!), but Leonardo did not spend much time being upset about all of this. Instead, he made corrections and went on about his business. Creative people are those who are willing to see something that doesn't work, make corrections, and get on with business. Too often, though, we bog down in protecting our point of view, having to be right, and sticking to something that isn't working long after we should have tried something else. We get copious cues from inside and outside ourselves when things aren't working, and if we ignore the first subtle cues, they will escalate in a more noticeable form. Often, though, instead of correcting we get scared and tighten up our defenses. Finally, the cues will escalate to the point where they are bashing us over the head. Then, correcting is a major effort.

PARENTS ARE PEOPLE TOO

Parents are in a paradoxical position in families. They are busy learning what works and what doesn't, and, to do this, they have to "unlearn" much of what they learned from their families when they were growing up. Much of what parents accepted as real, true, and useful turns out to be just beliefs, opinions, and biases passed down from their parents, who in turn got them from their parents. What's worse, most of these beliefs turn out not to work very well. Creative parents are those who are getting out from under the limiting beliefs and opinions from the past, and who are finding out what works now. In fact, creative people in general are those who ask themselves frequently, "What limiting beliefs are keeping me from responding well to this situation?"

Suppose, for example, that one of the beliefs a father had had instilled in him by his parents was "Big boys don't cry." This belief is one of the kind that doesn't work very well, because there are plenty of times in life, such as when you have lost someone or feel hurt, when crying is appropriate. If you believed the "don't cry" message, you wouldn't be able to respond to the situation effectively. So, a creative father who saw this belief at work in his life would see that it doesn't work and would go about the business of letting himself feel sad when that was what he felt.

CHILDREN AND PARENTS ARE PEOPLE

Since parents are having to learn it all from scratch, just like children, it would be helpful if we simply viewed both parents and children as people. As people, we all have the same needs, the same feelings, and the same essence. We are all in the process of learning together. Children need to know that their parents are learners, too. Parents need to get out from under their "I have to do it right" mentality to let their children see that they are struggling with the same issues they are. Creative parents are those who wake up to the fact that as their children grow, they are giving the parents a chance to work through all the unfinished business from their own childhoods. As children work on learning to meet their needs and deal with their feelings, parents have the magnificent opportunity to rework those same issues in themselves. One of the creative things children do is to approach life with a beginner's mind: Let's see what works. Parents who adopt this framework find that both life, and their children, become friendlier to them.

FAMILIES ARE PLACES WHERE WE LEARN HOW TO GET OUR NEEDS MET

All of us, parents and children, need the same things. If we learn how to get these needs met in straightforward ways, life can be simple and satisfying. If we don't know what these needs are, and if we have to learn crooked ways to meet them, life is complicated, scary and unhappy. Let's find out what some of these needs are so that we can see them in ourselves, respond to them in others, and learn to meet them straightforwardly.

WHAT WE NEED

In Western society, many of our basic physical needs are met: We have food, shelter, and clothing. Since these needs are often met, we can then turn our attention to psychological needs, which, when met, can help us flourish and reach our full potential.

First, we all need love. If we have experienced unconditional love, we have a psychological cushion under us for life. The problem is that much of the love we receive is the conditional kind: I'll love you if you'll . . . (be quiet, do things my way, be a cute little girl, lose some weight, etc.). The conditional kind of love makes us wary of all kinds of love so that later in life we may defend ourselves against even unconditional love when it is offered to us. If we do not know how to meet our need for love directly, we will play an infinite number of games to meet it crookedly.

Not only do we need love from others, but we also need to love ourselves deeply. Here we are not talking about egotism; egotism is an attempt to get the world to love you after you have ceased to love yourself. To love ourselves is to greet each part of us—our feelings, our thoughts, our bodies—with warmth and acceptance. Nearly every problem we humans experience can be traced to an inability to love some part of ourselves. If we do not love ourselves, we will demand love from the world around us. Yet, when we get it, it will not be satisfying. When we love ourselves, love naturally flows to us from the world.

We all need attention. Each one of us needs to have energy directed to him by others. Attention is one of the things humans thrive on. If we do not get our attention in straight ways, the crooked ways will abound. For one person, attention will be gained through getting ill; for another, the game will be to get attention through having accidents. A child will learn to get attention with a noisy temper tantrum, while another child, even in the same family, will do it by withdrawing and being shy.

We also deeply need a sense of self-worth. The sense of self-worth comes in two parts. First, we need a sense that we are loveable just for being here. Then, on top of that can come a sense of being able to *do* things in a workable manner. The sense of self that says, "I am basically loveable and okay" precedes the later sense of "I am capable." We need attention both for being and for doing. All of us need to have rewarding things to do. Finding something to do is a basic human need. Now, more than ever, when activities like watching television threaten to lull us into a passive posture, families need to be places where we can learn how to look around us for creative things to do.

We all need information and skills in living. To live a successful life, we absolutely must know some basic information about our feelings. We need to know that all our feelings have a place; it's okay to be sad, scared, happy, angry, and excited. We need to have alternative ways to handle those feelings so that we don't express feelings in ways that don't work. We also need to learn to think and to solve problems. Our minds are the most magnificent instruments in what we know of creation, yet we use only a limited range of our abilities.

We all need to grow. Some of our needs are for growing in self-knowledge; other needs are for growing in our sensitivity to others and our abilities to be with people. Humans also have a yearning for connection with the universe and a higher power. Families are places where these higher needs can be nurtured and allowed to blossom.

From the very rock-bottom basics, like meeting our needs for love and attention, to the highest possible needs, self-actualization, and transcendence, families can be our best teachers or our most formidable barriers to knowing how to meet our needs in clear, satisfying ways.

Let us look, for a moment, at what happens when our basic needs are or are not met.

DECIDING HOW THINGS ARE GOING TO BE

Families are places where we make our basic decisions about the way the world is and how we are going to be in the world. Our later lives are spent acting out those decisions or trying to remake them in the face of evidence that the decision is no longer workable.

It must be understood that these decisions are made because they are the most workable opportunity at the time. The decisions are made for security and even survival reasons and are often difficult to give up: Our very safety and survival has depended on them.

I Am Loveable

One of the most important decisions we make is whether or not we are loveable. Depending largely on the quality of our earliest contacts with people, usually our mother, we make crucial decisions about our basic life position of loveableness or unloveableness. If we decide that we are not loveable, that decision can color all of our experience and make us do outlandishly destructive and self-destructive things later when we experience stress in our lives. Families can provide essential nourishment for our growth by liberally dispensing positive messages about these basic decisions:

You deserve all the love in the world.

You are a loveable person.

You are loveable no matter how you feel.

No matter what you do, you deserve love.

We need to hear and feel these kinds of messages so that every cell in our bodies feels loveable. Parents and children alike are in the process of deciding that they are loveable. Almost none of us really feels loveable and worthwhile all the time. Remember, family life is a mirror that magnifies parents' unfinished business in the emotional domain. Creative parents use the development of their children to observe and remake decisions that are no longer serving them.

I Can Be Real

One of the fateful decisions that we make in our families is whether we can be real and still be loved. For many of us, our real feelings are rejected: We get in trouble if we express sadness, anger, fear, or our sexuality. Rejection doesn't make our feelings go away, of course. It simply drives them underground and teaches us that we cannot be real, that we must put on a mask to be accepted by others. Later in life, the very masks that worked in childhood become the barriers we must dissolve in order to be real.

I Can Trust

The decision about whether or not people can be trusted is an early decision that has deep influences on how we live our whole lives. Sometimes, because of negative childhood experiences, we may make a blanket decision not to trust. (Remember that our early decisions are made to protect us.) Ideally, we will see that we can trust certain people and not trust others; we will make the decision in each case based on available data. However, if we make a blanket "Don't Trust" decision, we take a wary life stance that prejudges every encounter as one in which we are likely to lose something. The result is that our encounters are shallow and unsatisfying. If we can learn early in life that it is all right to trust people until they give us indications otherwise, then we can take a more open stance toward life.

I Can Win

A most pervasive decision that is made by children and parents alike is whether or not they can win in their family. In most competitive situations, winning is defined as getting more than someone else. Here, though, we are talking about a different kind of winning, one in which everyone who plays can reach fulfillment. To win in life means to generate actions that have positive consequences for yourself while maximizing positive consequences for others. Any action that causes another person to experience negative consequences is not a winning action in the long run. One of the fundamental laws of the universe is that when you initiate actions that cause negative consequences for others, it will eventually circle back on you to trip you up.

Negative childhood experiences may put us in a position where an I-can't-win decision is the only workable alternative. In this case, we develop a number of life strategies for coping with the world from an I-can't-win position. Several of these strategies are:

> If I can't win, I'm just not going to play.
>
> If I can't win, I'm going to make damned sure nobody does.
>
> I'm going to take the ball and go home.

We absolutely have to help everyone in a family to know that everyone can win. We need to pass along messages like:

> We can solve problems so that everyone wins.
>
> Everyone can get his or her needs met here.
>
> In order for one of us to win, all of us have to win.

One of the major roadblocks to having families in which everyone can win is that sometimes parents (and occasionally children) have to be right all the time. Being right comes from being scared, and it doesn't work. One reason it doesn't work is that it automatically means someone else has to be wrong. In life, any situation in which one person wins and another loses is a loser.

A later chapter on problem solving will explain a number of ways to solve problems so that everybody wins.

I Can Feel and I Can Think

In families, we have a wonderful opportunity to learn how to feel and to think. Unfortunately, families are also one of the two major training grounds (along with schools) for stupidity and unfeelingness. Dozens of times in my counseling office I have seen how a family of vibrant and capable people has managed to turn one another into unthinking, rigid automatons.

We humans have a problem with giving one another space. We are deluded into thinking that being helpful is invading another's space and doing something to them or for them. In fact, real helpfulness is helping the person occupy the maximum amount of his or her space. In the realm of feelings, we may be around someone, perhaps a child, who is hurt. Instead of giving him or her the space to experience that feeling, we tend to jump in with

Be brave.

It'll be okay tomorrow.

Cheer up.

Don't be a baby.

Big boys don't cry.

Messages such as these, even though they may seem helpful, deny the person the space in which to have the experience he or she is having. Helpful reponses, such as

That must hurt.

I think I know how that must feel.

I'd like to hear more about it.

Help the person expand to be more aware of the space he or she occupies. Oftentimes, this is the only "help" that must be given, for it allows the person to complete the experience and move on or think of a workable solution. In counseling, I have seen many people solve what appeared to me to be nearly insurmountable problems by gradually exploring their feelings and expanding their territories of awareness. One of the miracles of life, in my opinion, is when a person comes up with a creative and workable solution to a problem that formerly seemed insoluble.

We need to give out many messages like:

It's okay to feel sad
　　　　　　angry
　　　　　　scared
　　　　　　excited
　　　　　　etc.

It's okay to be you.

You can think of and come up with a creative solution for that.

Let's give one another the space to feel whatever we're feeling.

We also need to observe the many ways we deny people space. Some of the common ways are:

Talking people out of feelings (e.g., There's nothing to be scared of, you'll feel better tomorrow).

Interrupting them.

Not listening.

Doing their thinking for them.

When we deny people space, we leave them few choices but to act defensively. If, however, we can give people in our families plenty of permission to feel and think, a richly vibrant and creative family can be ours.

SUMMARY

Families are magic mirrors. They magnify our feelings and needs. They let us see the old patterns we bring to them that are getting in the way of our being who we really are.

Families are where we learn to meet our basic needs. If we learn to meet them in crooked, game-playing ways that force us to mask our real selves, life becomes painful and unrewarding. When we learn to meet our needs directly, life is full of unparalleled satisfactions.

Families are where we make our basic decisions about how to be. For parents, family life becomes the magic mirror that allows them to see and remake old decisions that are no longer working. For children, family life is an opportunity to see if being real can bring them love, truth, and satisfaction. For all, the goal of families is to teach us how to be centered in word and deed and to give us enduring skills that will serve us throughout life.

2

how to transform
your family
through
clear communication

One of the key parts of growing a centered family is learning how to talk to one another. Clear communication is so valuable, so beautiful, and so very rare. Words can open us up to one another, letting our essence shine forth, or they can bury us in the mud of misunderstanding and misery. When we share who we really are, being human becomes touching and luscious. When we use words to obscure the us inside, being human is lonely and burdensome. Let us use this chapter as a way of finding out how we can talk to one another so that the real us (which is full of love, truth, and simplicity) can shine, and so we can learn how to nurture its luminescence in others.

As I begin this chapter, I am experiencing just how deeply I feel about good communication. It hurts me very much to see how we fail to make contact with one another. It hurts when I fail to be real and communicate clearly with my close ones. At those times I feel angry and hurt at my inability to find my own essence and see the essence in others. I see so clearly the damage that is done by not being clear with others. When I was growing up, feelings, needs, and expectations were not talked about openly.

27

So, they came out crookedly, in tense silence, sarcasm, threats, advice, and all the other tools of poor communication. I saw my grandparents, who were married 60 years, spend at least 20 of those years (the length of time I knew them) angry at each other without talking about it in a straightforward way. It was painful to me to watch all those fine people fail to communicate with one another. I, like other children, found myself often thinking something like "How can I get these people to accept themselves and deal with one another straight?" I found it difficult then and I find it difficult today—both with myself and others. Being real and sharing ourselves is at once extraordinarily simple and harder than anything we can imagine.

I often feel ecstatic when I am able to share a feeling, a fantasy, an old resentment, or a deep need with someone I'm close to. Really getting to the bottom of a negative feeling can be as exhilarating as sharing a positive feeling. I remember a time when my daughter, then 10, and I had been locking horns and making each other miserable for a week or so. Finally one night we were standing in the kitchen, glaring at each other after some snide exchange. I said, "I'm really angry." As soon as I said it, I felt something soften inside me. I was no longer able to hang on to the anger. She must have picked up what happened inside me by telepathy, for suddenly she said, "Dad, I just need to know if I can act my worst and you'll still love me." I told her that I needed to know that from her, too. Then we were both overcome with tears. When I hugged her, I felt as joyful as I did the first time I picked her up as a baby. After seeing it happen hundreds of times in my own life and in doing counseling with others,

I conclude that one way to make magic happen is to share something real in a straight way with another person.

WHAT WORKS
AND WHAT DOESN'T

Good communication is the art of going from the surface down to the deepest thing that's going on inside us. Some of the surface things we do to keep our inner experience covered up are:

silence

blaming

placating

threatening

giving advice

being reasonable

None of these things works very well; they are things we do until we find what works. What works is straight talk. Before we explore it, let's look at why those strategies mentioned above do not work.

Mainly, strategies like blaming or giving advice don't work because they do not deal with what is really going on inside us. Look at a typical blaming and placating situation:

On the surface, the two people are blaming and placating each other, which is ineffective and a losing situation for both. Deeper inside is where the real action is taking place. Her insides are probably saying,

"I'm scared and I feel unloveable."

"I feel tense and tired."

"I need reassurance that you care about me."

"I feel hurt and angry you forgot."

"My expectation was that you would bring me a present."

His insides are probably saying,

"I'm scared that you're gonna be mad at me."

"I'm angry that I messed up and I'm in trouble again."

"I'm tired and upset and need nurturing."

"I feel really bad that you don't feel loved."

"I feel unloveable right now, too."

The astounding thing about communication is that almost any of the deeper issues inside, if expressed, could transform the whole encounter. If one person will venture beneath the surface and deal with something real, magic can happen.

Let us also look at the deeper issues beneath that family favorite, advice-giving. Let us say, for example, that Dad is giving advice to his son about driving the family car. It's difficult to give advice without using words like *don't, should, never,* and *always.* The trouble is that these words cause most people to go temporarily deaf. Teenagers are particularly susceptible to this form of deafness. We have all heard so many pieces of useless advice that have these words in them that our minds automatically shut them out, even if the advice is good. So, is there another way to communicate the same information without giving advice? Yes, there is. We can circumvent poor communication strategies like blaming and advice giving by *sharing experience.*

SHARING EXPERIENCE

People listen when we share real experience. People don't listen as well when we share abstractions about experience. Advice is usually made up of abstractions about experience. It turns people off. If we want to turn them back on, we must share the experiences themselves.

Abstractions

Don't drive over the speed limit.

One should never drink and drive.

Always check your mirror.

Don't do anything stupid.

You should always come to a full stop at stop signs.

Underneath abstractions like these are real experiences that, if shared, will not only be heard but will transform the relationship.

Experiences

I'm scared that you'll get hurt or be in an
accident; I know that speeders have more
accidents.

I'm scared that you'll do something silly that
will hurt you or my car.

I got a ticket once for running a stop sign. It
cost me $25.

Once I got hit from behind by a drunk.

Once I had three beers before driving and I
almost hit a pedestrian.

When we share experiences, it lets the real us shine.
When we don't, we lose touch with ourselves, and people
lose interest in what we say.

STRAIGHT TALK IS WHAT WORKS

Straight talk is when what you are talking about matches
up with what is going on inside you. It is putting your
inner experience in the simplest possible terms.

STRAIGHT TALK
IS NOTHING FANCY

In good communication, our goal is to let others know us
without making them work at it too hard. When we catch

ourselves being fancy, we use that as a cue to make it simpler, to get back to the basics. Thus, a statement like

> I feel the way I did the time we had that big argument and you left me alone in downtown San Francisco.

is definitely fancy, and can be simplified to a straight-talk statement like

> I'm scared.

I remember doing marital counseling one day with a couple who were both therapists themselves. They intellectually "knew" all of what we are calling straight talk, but they were stuck and unable to put it into practice. In fact, when I kept trying to get them to make straight-talk statements to each other, they would look at me as if to say, "Aw, that stuff won't work with *us.*" I persisted, however, because I felt that their very problem was that they had become so sophisticated in their communications with each other that they were leaving the basics unsaid. Finally, after a painful half hour of tearing each other apart, they were able to make some straight talk with each other. They made eye contact and made statements like the following:

> I'm scared that you might leave me.
> I need more attention from you.
> I want your love.

I'm afraid of being alone.

I'm scared I'm too dependent on you.

I feel trapped.

When they were able to make contact with what was really going on deep inside themselves and were able to communicate this to each other, the tension in the room dissolved and turned into a kind of quiet joy. Then, we were able to generate some sound solutions to their problems.

We are all trying to learn that when we get out of touch with ourselves, we feel scared and alienated. Coming back into harmony with ourselves and talking about our inner experiences with those we are close to puts us back on a satisfying track.

Let's look at the components of straight talk. They're nothing fancy—just the stuff of real human experience.

TALK ABOUT YOUR FEELINGS

Perhaps the key skill in clear communication is learning how to talk about our feelings. We are all on a lifelong curriculum of learning to identify our feelings and talk about them. We know what happens if we don't share our feelings. We get lonely, our bodies get tense and may even get sick, or we will have bad dreams and unsettling fantasies. When we are out of touch with our feelings, and when we do not communicate them clearly to others, we become estranged from ourselves, our friends, and our family. Our interactions become full of the shallow babble that passes for conversation in most of our lives.

It is not difficult to tell when we are talking about feelings—there's only a handful of basic ones—but being able to talk about them in a straight way in the heat of the moment is a skill that requires much commitment and practice.

Take, for example, the feeling of *anger.* Anger is a basic feeling that comes up when we don't get something we want. We get superficially angry when we don't get something superficial, like a toy, but we get deeply angry when we don't get something we deeply want, like love or acknowledgment. One of the most important life skills is learning to express anger with straight talk.

I'm angry that _____ .

I got angry when _____ .

I felt angry at _____ .

When anger is expressed with that kind of clarity, it sets the stage for a resolution of the problem. However, anger is often expressed in a crooked way, with blame attached. Sometimes, blame is accompanied with a threat.

You make me so furious! I'll get you for that!

Why on earth did you do that?

If you do that again, I'll . . .

Crooked ways of expressing anger imply that the speaker is right and the other party wrong. No one ever solved a problem from that position. One of our human weaknesses is that we often put more energy into being right than we put into solving a problem. If we can gradually let go of our need to be right all the time, a dramatic increase in happiness will be ours.

People are a parfait of feelings; anger may be only the top layer. When we get below the surface, it often becomes apparent that the anger was covering a deeper feeling like hurt or fear. If we deal only with the anger, we may miss the real issue. So, when a problem arises, try on other feelings to see if they fit.

I'm scared that _____ .

I feel hurt when _____ .

I'm sad that _____ .

Straight talk works just as well with positive feelings. In fact, a good rule of thumb for family interactions is to make sure that the number of positive feelings you express at least equals the number of negative ones.

I feel good when _____ .

I felt happy when you _____ .

I felt so joyful when _____ .

I really liked it when _____ .

Acknowledging the positive, healthy things people do is an art that does not come automatically, so let us discuss acknowledgment for a moment.

GIVE FAMILY MEMBERS RICH AND FREQUENT ACKNOWLEDGMENT

Acknowledgment is when you:

Hug people.

Say something pleasant and supportive to them.

Listen to them carefully.

Tell them some reasons why you like them.

Thank them for something they did.

Tell them they did a good job on something.

Ask them to do something with you.

The opposite of acknowledgment, which I call *erosion* and which is all too prevalent in our society, is to:

Belittle people.

Be sarcastic.

Ignore them.

Be critical.

Interrupt them.

If we are to have a satisfying family life, it is absolutely essential that we make the family a place of rich, frequent acknowledgment. Further, we must set things up so that *erosion* is minimized.

Once, the Fates assigned me the task of driving a car packed full of kids ranging in age from seven to thirteen. While we were waiting to begin our trip to the beach, about an hour's drive away, I noticed that the level of erosion was unpleasantly high. It seemed that most of the interactions were put-downs of some sort; the kids who did not participate in the put-downs did not seem to say anything at all.

As I drove away, an idea occurred to me. I pulled over to the side of the road and made a little speech, something like:

> "I get upset when you folks say unpleasant things to one another. All of you seem like good people, and that's what I'd like you to support in one another. To help you, and to keep me happy, I'm going to pull over and stop the car if anyone says or does anything unpleasant. We'll resume our trip when that person apologizes and says something pleasant to balance it out."

They immediately tested me to see if I meant it. It took us 20 minutes to cover two blocks. After that, the atmosphere brightened and we had a delightful trip. They chatted happily about their lives, supporting and acknowledging one another in the spontaneous way kids can. I had the feeling that several of the kids had lived in an environment so full of erosion, and so deprived of acknowledgment, that our trip to the beach may have been the first time in their lives that the tables had been turned.

Unhealthy families arrange things so that people only get acknowledged when they are doing something hurtful to themselves or others. In some families, the only way to get nurturing acknowledgment is to get sick. We all need nurturing every day, and if we learn to get it in a straight way we will be able to generate much kindness toward us in our life. If we learn that we must get sick in order to be nurtured, we are likely to create much more illness in our lives than we ordinarily might.

Unhealthy families also arrange things so that inappropriate behavior is acknowledged. Family members are acknowledged when they throw a temper tantrum, hit someone, or put on an act. Remember, for someone who needs acknowledgment, there is little difference between positive and negative attention. For a child, both a hug and a slap constitute attention. There is an art to learning to acknowledge the positive, healthy things people do. It is an art that takes a lifetime to master, but we can all start where we are and begin to notice what we are acknowledging in our families.

MAKE EYE CONTACT AND GET BODY LANGUAGE CLEAR

When we talk to one another, it is important to make eye contact. The eyes are the windows to the soul, and since our task is to communicate our souls, we need to let our eyes be in communication. Also, we need to check ourselves to make sure our body language is saying the same thing that our words are saying. The impact of words is cancelled out when we do not support them with good eye contact and open body language.

COMMUNICATE
YOUR EXPECTATIONS

Feelings get dialed up when we have some expectation that isn't met. In getting our communication cleared up, it's important to get in touch with our expectations in various situations.

> My expectation is that you'll bring the car back clean and full of gas.
>
> I expect the job to be done thoroughly.
>
> My expectation is that we will talk about this without either of us storming out.

If the expectation is there but unspoken, there is an invitation to feel angry if it is not met.

EXPRESS YOUR WANTS
AND NEEDS

Things work better in our lives when we are clear with one another about what we want and need from one another. One psychologist estimated that 90 percent of all arguments could be prevented by the parties' putting their "argument energy" into figuring out what they want and need from one another.

Often we must begin with our surface wants to get to the deeper needs beneath. For example, a person who wants a certain car may want it because it meets a deeper need for self-esteem and power. The question then must be asked if when the surface want is attained (the car is purchased) the deeper need will be satisfied. Most often, the deeper need must be met directly: through acknowledgment of it, acceptance, and expression. When we try to meet deep needs with *things*, we are likely to end up with a lot of things, but with a deeper feeling of dissatisfaction.

It is not easy to get in touch with what we want and need. First, few of us put much thought into what we really need. Then, we are talked out of our wants in the growing-up process and often are taught to meet our needs in crooked ways. When we can get clear on what we want and need and express our wants and needs to others, our lives are often transformed.

Instead of using our energy to define what we *don't want* and complain about what we *don't have*, let us try to put forward our wants and needs positively. This approach can work with material wants as well as deeper wants and needs. Here are some examples of positively phrased wants and needs.

I want a comfortable, reliable car for under $6,000.

I want to feel a deep sense of self-respect and self-esteem.

I need love.

I need to feel safe and secure.

I want you to be here when I come home.

I want you to tell me more often that you love me.

I want you to be quiet and polite in the grocery store today.

I want one or more friends with whom I can share stimulating conversation.

Parenting goes much easier when parents can remember to be clear about what they want from children. Kids need to know what is expected of them, what the limits are, and what the rules of the game are. If these things are made clear to children beforehand, much troublesome behavior can be avoided.

The same principles hold true for other family relationships, such as that between husbands and wives. When they can tell each other clearly what they want and need for themselves and from each other, it takes the guesswork out of being close. In relationships between parents, or between parents and children, an ounce of prevention is easily worth a pound of cure.

SHARE YOUR JOURNEYS WITH ONE ANOTHER

Each of us is on a quest: to learn about ourselves, about relating to one another, about the universe. Often we do not acknowledge the dramatic nature of this quest to ourselves; less often do we talk with one another about our journeys. Yet, one of the things that seems to bring people closest is when they share their journeys.

Some of my most satisfying conversations with my close ones have been when I have talked to them about my journey: the issues I was dealing with, the feelings I was trying to understand and accept, the difficulties I was having trying to be real and express myself. When I am not feeling close to, say, my daughter, what brings us closer is usually taking a walk or having dinner together and sharing those kinds of things with each other. I find that I usually take the lead; rarely does she initiate those kinds of deeper conversations. When I share with her, though, it nearly always elicits fascinating discussions of what is going on in both of our lives and minds.

Sometimes in a family the conversations about deeper issues only take place when there is a problem or crisis. We also need to make time to talk about what is important to us when there is not as much emotion in the air.

EXPERIMENTS IN FAMILY COMMUNICATION

Here are some suggestions for activities that I have seen work to improve family communication.

   1. *Have a Family Feelings Meeting.* In a Feelings Meeting, the rules are simple: Each person states how he or she feels or felt and describes briefly what might have triggered that feeling. All basic feelings are covered, and no discussion or feedback is allowed until a later agreed-upon time. The following structure can be used for each feeling-statement:

I feel (or felt) _____ when _____ .

The basic feelings to be covered are: angry, scared, hurt, happy. Here are some sample statements:

I felt mad Tuesday. Nothing happened, I just got up feeling that way.

I feel sad that Jim's gone to camp.

I felt scared when Daddy yelled at me.

I felt angry when Ted broke the lamp.

I am angry at Mark for having such a messy room.

I felt hurt when Bobby told me to shut up.

I feel happy when you kids are playing together in a friendly way.

It is important in a Feelings Meeting that each person gets a chance to talk about all of the basic feelings without criticism. In a Feelings Meeting, no criticism should be given about whether a feeling is justified, right, bad, or good. It is simply a chance for everyone to give voice to things he or she is feeling or has felt.

2. *Have a Family Wants Meeting.* In a Wants Meeting, the idea is to share things that family members want for themselves and from one another. It is often best to start with material wants.

> I want a 10-speed bike.
>
> I want a new camper.
>
> I want a bigger refrigerator.
>
> I want an increase in my allowance.

Then you can proceed to deeper wants.

> I want more hugs from you.
>
> I want some free time each day.
>
> I want you to stop telling me to shut up; I want you say "be quiet" instead.
>
> I want to spend more time planning how we spend our weekends.

In a Wants Meeting, no criticism is allowed, and no effort is made to edit the wants to make them more realistic or reasonable. Obviously, all wants will not be acted upon. It is simply an opportunity for family members to clear out their minds.

Both Feelings and Wants Meetings can teach valuable lessons. It teaches us to state our feelings and wants clearly. It lets us do it with no criticism or punishment. And it lets us know that we do not have to act on each feeling or want that is contributed; we are simply given the space to have the feeling or want.

3. *Have a "What Works" Meeting.* It is important in life to learn to identify what of our behavior works and what doesn't. Some of our behavior can be seen by ourselves; other aspects must be brought to our attention by others. If it is brought to our attention in ways that we perceive to be threatening, our tendency is to become defensive. We need to structure the situation so that we do not need to protect ourselves. The "What Works" Meeting is a way to structure feedback so that correction, rather than protection, is the result.

The way to conduct a "What Works" Meeting is to have family members call attention to behavior and its consequences. Explanations and rationalizations are avoided; discussion is held for a later time. The focus is on identifying as much behavior as possible.

Here are examples of statements made during a "What Works" Meeting.

> It isn't working for you to leave your room so messy. People keep hassling you.
>
> It isn't working for you and Dad to discuss money. You end up in a fight every time.
>
> It works when you and Allan help and say nice things to each other. Good things seem to happen after that.
>
> It doesn't work for you to have your friend Steve over to study with you. You end up distracting each other and being reprimanded for making too much noise.

It really seems to work when we all spend time together at night without the TV on. We almost always have a nice time.

A major contribution that families can make to our mental health is skill in helping us see what aspects of our actions work and which ones do not. The family "What Works" Meeting can be a step in that direction.

3

how to solve problems
and build responsibility

The art of growing a centered family involves starting from where we are and lovingly dissolving the barriers to feeling centered. One of the major barriers is learning how to handle the problems that occur in families. Problems occur in all families; that is the way it is. If we accept that fact and work with it, instead of resisting it, we can turn the very problems that haunt us into experiences in centering. In other words, we can stop seeing problems as "problems" and start seeing them as opportunities to learn about ourselves and how we can handle the world from a more loving stance. There are ways of solving problems that also teach self-esteem and build responsibility; this chapter discusses several specific strategies for doing that. Our focus in this chapter is on what works, not what suits some elegant theory. There are probably other problem-solving strategies that work well, but I will focus on ones that I have seen work to help families solve real problems.

FEELINGS FIRST,
SOLUTIONS LATER

One common error many of us make in solving our problems is that we rush to solutions before deeply understanding the problem. A good rule of thumb is to hear everyone's feelings thoroughly before beginning to look for a solution. A bonus of this approach is that many problems will clear up automatically by simply carefully hearing everyone's point of view. We need to avoid the trap of thinking we need to *do* something with every problem. Often, just *being* with it is enough.

All feelings must be considered. Consider, for example, an argument between a 12-year-old girl and her 11-year-old brother. The surface argument is that they each think the other is doing less of the kitchen chores. Each is angry and has cited many examples of kitchen inequity. If they were able to make clear statements of their *anger,* they might say:

> He: I'm angry that I have to do more work.

> She: I'm angry that you do less work than I do.

But if we look beneath the surface anger, we might see things they are *scared* about:

> He: I'm scared I'm not getting as much as you.
>
>   I'm scared that I'm not getting as much love and attention as you are.

I'm scared because I see you happy a lot of the time, and I don't feel as good about myself. I'm afraid I'm a loser.

She: I'm afraid I'm not getting the love and attention that you're getting. I'm afraid that since I'm older Mom always expects more of me. I'm afraid I can't handle it.

For the sake of example, I have presented very clear statements of deep issues. It would be rare to get these kinds of statements of feeling without a little bit of work.

So, what looked on the surface like an argument about kitchen chores turned out to be a manifestation of children's normal fears about whether they are going to get enough love, whether they can live up to expectations, and whether they are equipped to handle the world. Acknowledging and expressing those fears would most likely clear up the kitchen problem entirely. If it did not, the problem would at least be approached from a more centered place. Our main point here, though, is that a solution to a problem will often spontaneously emerge if we consider all parties' feelings first.

Problem solving is tricky because people have different points of view. In other words, we all view a problem from slightly different angles. The way I think of it is that we each have a different snapshot of a problem. Before we solve it, we have to be given space to show our snapshot—our particular view—of the situation. Once we are assured that our snapshot is a valid and valued one, we can then consider another person's point of view. It is this act of feeling good about our point of view and then giving it up and looking at someone else's that contributes much to solving a problem.

SETTING LIMITS IS IMPORTANT

Many problems can be dissolved by making it clear what the limits are. All of us have limits. Most are reasonable. If we bring them out into the open and discuss them, they can always be modified. But if we keep them to ourselves, it is a set-up for us to get upset when the limits are violated. It does a particular favor for children when parents set limits. Inside, kids are always asking the question "How does this part of the world work?" Setting limits lets them know in advance what the rules of that particular area of the world are.

HOW TO SET LIMITS
WITH CHILDREN

The best time to set limits is in advance (rather than in retreat!). If we wait until the heat of an argument, our limits are often contaminated by the feelings we are having and do not accurately reflect our true limits.

The basic limit-setting procedure with children is to tell them clearly what you want from them, what makes you upset, and what your expectations are. Take, for example, a mother of two children who wants to spend some time alone in her room each day but keeps being interrupted by the children. She might say:

> It's important for me to have some time for me in the afternoon each day. I want to be by myself for 25 or 30 minutes about this time. I get angry when I'm interrupted, and then I get scared that I'm not ever going to have any time to myself. I expect you to play quietly and without interrupting me, unless there is an emergency, like if someone is hurt or there is an accident. Do you have any problems with that?

Here, the mother thoughtfully told the children her feelings and what she wanted, and she did it in a positive way. In a family, it is important to let the number of *dos* at least equal the number of *don'ts*. In other words, when we are clear with children about what we want from them, it will often prevent us from repeatedly telling them what we don't want. My rule of thumb is that one *do* is worth a dozen *don'ts*. Not only is it more effective to set positive limits with children, but it is also a lot more pleasant.

I have learned about limit setting the hard way, thrashing it out with my own child as well as with families in counseling. When she was two (heaven help all parents of two-year-olds) I took Amanda to the store quite a bit. We lived in the mountains, and the trip to the store every day or two was not only for provisions and mail, but also the main chance for socializing. Twice she threw tantrums in the store because I wouldn't get her something. I was embarrassed and angry at her, and I found myself chewing her out thoroughly after each occasion. Then it occurred to me that I was putting all my energy after the fact in telling her what I didn't want her to do. I decided to try it the other way around. So the next couple of times we went to the store I talked to her on the way about how I'd like her to be. I told her that it upset me to see her upset, and that I wanted her to be quiet and polite. I also told her I'd like her to be cheerful if she felt like it. If she wanted something, ask quietly for it, once only, and if I said no it was for some good reason and to be satisfied with it. She got the message and did exactly as I had asked. Then, I arranged it so her new behavior paid off. She asked for a penny sucker, so we bought it. I was pleased and made sure I told her so. The semi-happy ending of the story is that we've had no more problems in stores except for one small incident when she was about eight.

One harried single parent I know asked my advice after a disastrous party with his teenage daughter and her friends. During the party he had become upset when they played music too loud, danced too close, and made excursions out into the yard to do "Lord knows what," in his words. I advised him to invite his daughter to throw another party soon. When he recovered from the shock, I explained what I meant. I thought it would be good to throw another party so that he could make his limits clear. I helped him establish meaningful limits, and I also helped him get clear on some of his feelings about his daughter. Some of his feelings were:

> Anger that she had let her friends do things he disapproved of.

Fear that she was going to get into some kind of trouble.

Fear that she was getting out of his control.

Fear that she didn't know how to protect herself in the world.

Some of his limits were:

Everybody stays in the house.

Music no louder than 6 on his stereo.

No running in the house.

Lights on at all times.

Clean up the mess afterward.

About six weeks later they had another party, which was successful from both daughter's and father's points of view. They also learned a key lesson: It is possible to solve problems in such a way that everybody wins.

BASIC PROBLEM-SOLVING STRATEGY #1

The idea of a problem-solving strategy is to provide a set of step-by-step activities that we can use for a guide when problems occur. It can be useful to learn one or two healthy ways of solving problems because most of us bring to our relationships a lack of good information on how to solve problems in ways such that everybody can win. Some unhealthy ways of solving problems are:

coercing

threatening

changing the subject

invoking proverbs and authorities

The above kinds of strategies may cause a short-term reduction of the problem, but they will not get to the deeper issues that need to be resolved if the resolution is going to be lasting and meaningful. Our first basic problem-solving strategy has been found to be very useful in providing short- and long-term solutions to large and small problems.

Step 1: Commit Yourself to Listening

Sometimes just listening well to a problem will clear it up. This is because some problems occur because people have not had the recent experience of being heard. We all seem to be looking for understanding and acceptance, and if we do not get these things, problems will begin to appear. If listening does not bring a final resolution to the problem, at least it will set the stage for a resolution.* So, we need to make a lifelong commitment to becoming

*Readers who want to enhance their listening skills will find much valuable information in Thomas Gordon's books. Two of these are *Parent Effectiveness Training* and *Teacher Effectiveness Training*.

effective listeners if we are to become accomplished problem-solvers.

One extraordinarily effective listening technique is to have each person restate the other person's point of view before starting his or her own point. This technique ensures that each person has at least heard and understood the other's point.

Step 2: Get the Feelings Out First

A major step in solving problems is to create an opportunity for people to air any feelings they have collected. The deeper the feelings that are dealt with, the deeper and more thorough the resolution will be.

Anger is usually the feeling that is on the surface. This is because anger is dialed up any time we do not get what we want, and a problem is generally a situation in which people are not getting what they want. In a problem situation, people are (usually) also scared. In fact, some psychologists define fear as being in a situation for which we do not have a problem-solving strategy. Too, sadness is often part of a problem. People may have been hurt somewhere along the line and may not have had a chance to acknowledge and express it. So, the problem becomes an opportunity to discharge the energy built up from the unexpressed feelings of anger, hurt, or fear.

For example, a father and his teenage son may be arguing about the use of the car. Father's point of view is that the son has already been out several times during the week. Son's point of view is that he doesn't get to use the car as much as his friends. Let's look at what some of the surface feelings may be:

Father

Anger at being interrupted from reading paper.

Anger at having the same issue come up again in the same week.

Anger at having son speak to him negatively.

Son

Anger at not being able to go where he wants to go.

Anger at father not understanding him.

But if we look beneath the surface, we are certain to see deeper feelings going on:

Father

Scared that son will get into trouble.

Scared that they will never be able to solve problems effectively.

Hurt that they do not have a better relationship.

Son

Scared that he will not get the freedom and independence he needs.

Scared that his self-esteem will suffer in relation to friends.

Hurt that he is not understood.

Hurt that he can't get a good relationship with father.

We could say, then, that the car problem is a red flag that was sent up to call their attention to the deeper issues that needed to be dealt with. If the problem is dealt with only on the surface (anger/car) then a remarkable opportunity will have been missed to resolve some key issues and deepen the relationship. Our best bet is to regard problems as a surface manifestation of some deeper issue that is trying to be expressed. If we can look for a deeper issue and cannot find it, perhaps the problem can be solved at face value. But if we do not look deeper, we will not have the reward, for example, of looking beneath an angry family-power struggle and finding a struggle for love. For a look at some of the deeper issues that are trying to be resolved as children grow up, see the later section on child-developmental stages. Remember, too, that parents rework their own childhood unfinished business as their children pass through each developmental stage, so that, for example, parents of a two-year-old have the opportunity to rework their own unresolved problems from the two-year-old stage.

We might regard listening and getting the feelings out as steps that clear space around a problem. The bonus, of course, is that many problems are created because people have collected some feelings and are not listening to one another, so that to listen and air the feelings dissolves the problem. If the problem is still there after thoroughly listening and dealing with the feelings, the third step in the strategy usually clears up what is left over.

Step 3: Finding Out What People Want

Beneath any problem and any set of negative feelings is a set of things people want from others. If we put these wants out front, many problems will clear up. Although it sounds simple, many people have difficulty figuring out and clearly stating exactly what it is that they want.

A major barrier is that in a problem situation we are usually angry and scared, so we are not thinking clearly. At such a time, it is much easier to state what we don't want than it is to state what we want. That is why we must deal with feelings first. In humans, feelings occur at a deeper level than thinking, so feelings need to be dealt with before the thinking apparatus will work properly.

In stating wants, it is important to state them clearly, positively, and freely. Often we tend to edit our wants because we think they are unrealistic, silly, or unattainable. Editing them limits us; we must first get all of our wants out in the open. The unrealistic ones will naturally dissolve. We can consider a want to be stated clearly and positively if it looks something like the following:

I want more positive attention from you.

I want a chance to talk to you.

I want you to guarantee me you'll be careful.

I want your help with the dishes.

I want to know that you love me.

I want more time to myself.

I'd like the car Friday night.

I want to stay up later tonight to work on
my art project.

All of the above wants are stated clearly and positively. To be in touch with our wants in a situation seems to contribute as much to the solution of a problem as good listening and discussing feelings.

There are some practical considerations that make it easier to get in touch with both feelings and wants. Parents who are intervening in a heated dispute between children can separate the children for a while until they cool down enough to think. If children, for example, are sent to their rooms until they can write down how they are feeling and what they want, it can cut down the household-noise level for a while.

When working with people in counseling, I often have them close their eyes and repeat "I feel _____" and "I want _____" a number of times in their minds. I also have them jot down different wants between sessions so that they can remember them when we are together. After people have cleared up their feelings and wants inside themselves, I find it useful to have them make eye contact with one another and state their feelings and wants to one another. Magic seems to happen when we make contact with others and communicate deep things like feelings, wants, and needs.

The central premise of this first problem-solving strategy is that problems are generated when people store up feelings and when they have not figured out what they want from one another. Becoming clear on feelings and wants opens up a space for the resolution to occur.

BASIC PROBLEM-SOLVING STRATEGY #2

Our second problem-solving strategy is based on the idea that people have a built-in ability to solve problems. That is, we all have everything we need to solve our problems, but we sometimes get stuck and forget that we are capable and resourceful. This strategy provides a key we can turn to set our natural capabilities in motion.

As an example, let's say that a mother is consulted by her 9- and 10-year-old sons, who are fighting over which TV show they are going to watch. In this strategy the problem-solver—in this case the mother—takes full responsibility for understanding the problem and places full responsibility for solving it just where the responsibility belongs—on the children.

Son #1: It's not fair. Tommy always gets to watch what he wants. I never get to see the shows I want. I want to watch *Star Trek*.

Son #2: No, Mom! Dave watched *Star Trek* yesterday. Today it's my turn. I want to watch *The Big Movie*. Besides, I'm going to Bob's house tonight and I won't get to watch anything!

For Mom, it is a classic double-bind situation: No matter what kind of ruling she makes in the matter, she will be considered wrong by one party or the other. So, she avoids the Rescue Trap of providing a solution and simply describes the problem. This is a key step because it is an important function of families to help children see that they can think and solve problems creatively. It also keeps her from reasoning with the children. As any parent of 7- to 12-year-olds knows, children are master logicians and can counter any argument put up by a mere adult. So, clearly, reasoning is not the way either.

What would Mom say to the children to understand and describe the problem, but to avoid the Rescue Trap and the Let's Be Reasonable Trap?

There are dozens of ways to handle it. One way would be:

Mom: I understand that both of you are angry and want to watch different shows. I'd like you to turn off the TV and talk it over until

you come up with a solution that both of
you feel good about. Come talk it over with
me when you come up with something
so I can be sure everybody feels good.

Here, she listened and understood, but left the solution squarely on the people who created the problem. Too often, parents and teachers fall into the Rescue Trap and get maneuvered into doing kids' thinking for them. One of the very best uses we can make of problems is to see them as opportunities to help people learn to solve problems in ways that all parties win.

I put myself on a Rescue Diet about five years ago, and it has transformed my personal life as well as my work. I saw that many things I did came out of a Rescue mentality. With my daughter, with therapy clients, with my students, and with assorted other people in my life, I stepped into the Rescue Trap frequently. A student would come in to talk about a project, and I would give 90 percent of the suggestions. My daughter would tell me problems and I would fret over them. Then I woke up to what I was doing and started looking at how the tendency to rescue manifested in various areas of my life. I began redefining my role from providing solutions to helping people free up and clarify their own solutions.

Here are several examples from different areas of my life. One day in therapy I listened as a person described a very difficult problem regarding a decision he had to make. I described it back to him, asking him for more information and helping him get out more of his feelings. Then, when I got his assurance that I understood the problem, I asked him what he thought he ought to do. Without hesitating, he spelled out an ingenious course of action that I had not thought of. It came out so spontaneously that we both laughed. He said, "I wonder why I hadn't thought of that before?" I think it was because he had not put the problem out into the air, to let it breathe and be understood. When he had been listened to thoroughly, a solution popped up effortlessly.

I noticed that one of the games that my daughter and I played was that she would ask me what she could do for recreation that day. I would then rattle off a number of suggestions, which she would poke holes in. Then we would get angry at each other. So, I stopped doing that and began letting her do the thinking. Here is my recollection of a recent Saturday's dialogue.

Amanda: What should I do today?

Dad: That's a good question. I like to figure out what I'm going to do in the morning, too. How do you feel?

Amanda: Oh, sort of tired.

Dad: The kind of tired you get from getting too much exercise or too little?

Amanda: Too little. I've been just sitting around watching TV. I want to get outdoors.

Dad: What would you do?

Amanda: I think I'll go over and see if Heidi wants to skateboard.

These kinds of interactions really please me because I get the satisfaction of being helpful to people without robbing them of their ability to think for themselves. This style of problem solving works well in adult-to-adult interaction, too. Once in my university job I got a memo from the dean telling me that there was only enough money to fund half of a project I wanted to do. In our meeting I used the strategy I just described by doing my best to understand his point of view. I said things like:

> I see that the budget has been cut.
>
> I understand that we have only $2,000.
>
> It's hard having to cut back on worthwhile projects.
>
> It's a tough decision for you.

Then, I said,

> My problem is that I really want to do it.
>
> I'm committed to some students.
>
> This work will help out with some problems next fall.

So, I described his problem and my problem as thoroughly as I could. Before I finished, he broke in with a solution. By pulling a little money from here and a little from there, and by getting me to trim all the excess fat from my project, he came up with a workable solution for both of us. Before our talk we had both felt bad; afterward we both felt good.

A mother I know came up with what I felt to be a creative and thoughtful solution to a couple of problems that crop up in many families. Because it illustrates many of the points we have been discussing, I asked her to write up the process she went through to come to the solution.

One aspect of family life that has been very important to me as a parent is helping my children gain a sense of their own self worth by assuming as much responsibility for themselves as they are able at each stage of their development. Household tasks that are done by the child on a regular basis have been one part of this program. Each child has responsibility to the household and is relied upon to carry out that responsibility well and consistently. Over the years, tasks have changed and the structure around which responsibilities are organized has changed according to the development of the children.

It's easy to tell when the system needs to be changed. The old system will simply stop working. Suddenly a smoothly functioning household will become chaotic. I generally judge the timing for introducing a new system by my own level of frustration and how much nagging I find myself doing.

Recently it became apparent that I wasn't having much fun at home and so considered trying a new system. The children were complaining that the old system wasn't fair, and I was feeling that I suddenly had to do my job and everyone else's as well.

My children were 11 and 12 at the time and at a stage where it seemed important for them to learn more about cooperation and how they benefit personally from being responsible to other people. My basic premise was that if everyone takes part, we all have a better living environment and more time for fun with one another.

The first thing I did was to write down all the things that needed to be done in order to have a household that functions. A partial list of things that need to be done at my house is as follows:

1. Make the money to pay for food, clothing, shelter, and other things we need.

2. Pay the bills on time.

3. Do the dishes.

4. Water the lawn.

5. Clean the bedrooms.

6. Shop for groceries.

7. Iron the clothes.

8. Prepare meals.

9. Respect the rights of others.

10. Water the plants.

11. Take responsibility for the well-being of the family; think of ways to solve problems and get things done.

12. Take people places they need to go when they don't have transportation.

My list was about three times this long when I got finished. I also wrote down the things that I wanted to get from being a part of the family. This list included things like:

1. Good meals on time.
2. Time for fun with other family members.
3. Time for self.
4. A pleasant environment to be in.

I decided that I was not going to be able to make judgments about apportioning these jobs that both children would consider fair, so when we all sat down together, I told them that I had made a list of what I wanted to get from family life and a list of what jobs needed to be done to help the family function well. I then asked them to decide how these jobs should be divided up. They were to come up with a plan and present it to me for approval.

As the first howls of protest arose, I retired to my room to catch up on some reading. Half an hour later the children came in with their plan. They had given each task energy points ranging from one to three and divided up the responsibilities into those for me, those for each one of the children, and those that all of us should be responsible for. The abridged list looked something like this:

Mom (Total points: 17)

1. Pay the bills. (3 pts)
2. Make the money. (3 pts)
3. Take people places. (2 pts)

Susie (Total points: 13)

1. Water the lawn. (3 pts)
2. Do the dishes. (2 pts)

Steve (Total points: 15)

1. Water plants. (1 pt)

Everyone (Total points: 25)

1. Shop for groceries. (2 pts)
2. Clean own bedroom. (3 pts)
3. Iron. (1 pt)
4. Respect the rights of others. (2 pts)
5. Take responsibility for family well-being. (3 pts)

I was very pleased when I reviewed their work. Jobs were apportioned fairly according to energy points and appropriately acc ording to the capabilities of each family member. The children were willing to take responsibility for many intangible areas to contribute to total family well-being. The complete lists of each person's responsibilities and a weekly schedule that we we worked out together are posted on the refrigerator for everyone to refer to. If things are not done, we all know who's responsible.

CONCLUSION

Problems are opportunities to learn key life skills. We can use problems to help people understand and express their feelings, help them think creatively, figure out their wants and needs, and see how the world works. When problems are solved effectively, everybody wins. Seeing that we can set up our lives so everybody wins is one of the very best things our families can teach us.

meditation,
relaxation,
and centering activities
for the whole family

Families are always *doing* things together: eating, bowling, driving, arguing. This is good, because doing things together is one of the functions of families. But often we get so busy doing things that we forget about the importance of *being* together. Being together is when we are learning about ourselves and others, expanding our senses of self, and learning to resonate with the deeper aspects of each other. It would be nice if we could use all of our *doing* to also expand our *being*. That way, our whole lives could be a conscious process of growing more sensitive to ourselves and others. So often, though, our activities get us so caught up in them that we do not use them as opportunities to grow. So it is helpful to set aside some time every day or two for families to engage in activities that enhance their ability to *be* together.

In this chapter we will discuss ways of being together that involve meditating, relaxing, centering, and other ways of unifying mind, body, and spirit.

There are many reasons for doing activities like these on a regular basis in families. One reason is to strengthen family bonds. Many of the differences that keep us from feeling close to one another exist only on the surface of the mind. On the surface of the mind are all our painful thoughts:

Joey gets more than I do.

Nobody loves me.

I'm a real stumblebum.

When we do meditating, relaxing, and centering activities, we dip below the surface and explore the deeper parts of ourselves. When we get below the surface, differences disappear. We find that we all have the same deep feelings and needs. When we get very deeply into ourselves, we find that we are all one. We are all equal parts of the ocean of life and consciousness. Families who explore these depths together create a sense of harmony within and among themselves that builds a family bond at a level much deeper than that of words.

In addition, there is growing indication that activities like these are excellent ways of dissolving stress. Physicians are attributing more and more illness to stress these days. Many psychological problems are also caused by stress. Learning to calm the mind and body through meditating, relaxing, and centering activities may be as important to the future well-being of family members as learning good nutrition and hygiene habits.

PRACTICAL SUGGESTIONS

Out of doing these activities with my own family and in workshops with several thousand people over the last few years, I have collected some practical suggestions that enhance the effectiveness of the activities.

First, it is all right to start small. I suggest setting aside about 10 minutes at first, preferably at the same time each day. The time will naturally expand if the activities are valuable to the family. Before dinner is a good time, as is partway through the evening. I don't recommend doing the activities just before bedtime, with the exception of several activities described later that can be used to help people get to sleep. If the family has regular times each week for family meetings and discussions, many of the following activities can be built into the meeting. People think and express themselves more clearly after meditating or relaxing together.

No special postures or equipment is necessary for any of the activities. Most are done seated; some are done lying down.

Everyone should participate. Children and parents can take turns leading the activities. All directions are given in such a way that they can be read directly to the participants.

Meditating Together

Meditation is a way of quieting ourselves so that we can get to know ourselves at deeper levels and dissolve the barriers that are between us and our full potential. It is a way of relaxing mind and body so that they can learn to work in harmony. Sometimes meditation involves closing the eyes and focusing on an internal sound, sometimes it involves picturing an image, and sometimes it is just paying attention to your breath or the thoughts that pass through your mind. There are dozens of kinds of meditation available, so it is just a matter of picking one you like and doing it regularly.

Judging from my own experience—meditating about an hour a day since 1973—I believe that meditation should be done regularly to achieve its maximum benefits. Before I began meditating regularly my growth was positive but choppy, like a sputtering car that was slowly picking up speed. Once I began meditating on a daily basis, it felt like taking off smoothly in a jet.

There are commercial meditation organizations available in most cities. One of the best known is the Transcendental Meditation organization, which teaches an excellent technique using a *mantra*, or internally re-peated sound. They have a family plan in which all members of a family can learn for one fee. Although the fee is not cheap, the proceeds go to support an organization that you can then use to get your practice checked should you ever forget your mantra (!) or have any other dif-ficulties. The organization also presents introductory lectures on meditation that are informative and take a lot of the mystery and jargon out of the process.

Much of the time our inner sense of self is obscured. Thoughts, like memories, fantasies, and chatter, keep our minds busy and cluttered. Our bodies are full of feel-ings, sensations, and tension. These things are so noisy that it makes it hard to get in touch with the deep parts of ourselves. Meditation can help clear away these bar-riers. A tree, if it sends its roots down deep enough, can be nourished by a deep underground river. Families who meditate together find meditation to be as nourishing to their emotional, mental, and psychological growth as good food is to their physical growth.

FAMILY MEDITATIONS

Meditation #1—Getting Quiet Together

Here is a quick and simple meditation for families to use to get started in meditation. The instructions can be understood by children down to about 2½ years old. If you have a baby you would like to meditate with, sit him or her on a lap or near to you.

One good way to meditate together is to sit in a small circle or semicircle. Some families like to hold hands for a few minutes before beginning meditation. Use chairs or the floor to sit on, whichever you find more comfortable.

INSTRUCTIONS

"This meditation gives your mind something simple to focus on so that it can quiet down and get calm. We will focus on your breathing. Pick a place where you can feel the breath coming in and out of your body. Maybe it's your nose, maybe your chest. Just notice the breath coming in and out of you for a moment."

[Pause 10-15 seconds.]

"You'll notice that sometimes you'll be right with the breath, fully aware of it, then you'll be off thinking of something else. Your mind will wander and jump around quite a bit. Whenever you find your mind doing something else, just gently return it to your breathing. You may do this a lot of times or just a few times; either way it's okay. Now we'll meditate for a little while together."

[Start with 5-10 minutes; work up to 15-20 minutes.]

[When it's time to end:]

"Now just sit easily for a minute or two and turn your thoughts to the outside. Then, after a minute or two, gently open your eyes."

When divers have been exploring the ocean depths, they take a little time to come back to the surface. For the same reason, it is quite important to take a minute or two to come out of meditation. If you come out of meditation too quickly you may feel a bit out of sorts. If this should happen, close your eyes again for another minute or two until the feeling passes.

Meditation #2—Deeper Into the Quiet

Once you have explored being quiet together for a little while, you may want to go a little deeper into the workings of your minds and bodies. This series of instructions leads to a calm, clear, self-aware mind. It allows families to resonate together on a deep, nonverbal level.

INSTRUCTIONS

"Sit upright and comfortable. You can either close your eyes or keep them slightly open and resting on a spot in front of you."

[Pause 5–10 seconds.]

"In this meditation, we simply pay attention to the breath as it comes in and out of your body. Then when the mind wanders, we make a note of where it has wandered, then return to your breath. This lets you find out what goes on in your mind. For example, if you find yourself replaying a memory from yesterday or anytime in the past, make a mental note, 'memory,' then return to being aware of breath. Do the same when you find talk going on in your mind. Just make a mental note, 'talking,' and go back to the breath. Do the same with fantasy. If you find yourself playing a fantasy, something that hasn't really happened to you, make a note and return to the breath."

[Practice the preceding instruction for several days before going on to the following supplemental activity.]

"You've been exploring your mind recently by noting when it was playing fantasies, memories, or talk. Keep doing that now, and add to it the awareness of feelings. Sometimes all we notice is that a feeling is pleasant or unpleasant; other times you notice that it is one of the deeper emotions, like fear, sadness, anger, or joy. Pay attention to your breath, then if your mind wanders to your body, make a note of what you're aware of. Note 'pleasant' or 'unpleasant,' or you can note 'fear,' 'anger,' 'sad,' 'happy.' Then return to your breath after you've noted what you were feeling. So now we are noting things in your mind, like memory, fantasy and talk, plus feelings in your body."

[After a few days with the preceding instruction, you can add the following supplement:]

"Recently we have been getting quiet inside and noticing different events in the mind and body. Continue to note all the things that you remember from before,

memories
fantasies
talking
feelings,

and now note when you are using one of your senses. If you find your mind listening to something, make a note of 'hearing.' If you are aware of the feeling of the chair, note 'touching.' Do the same with 'seeing,' 'smelling,' and 'tasting.' "

Meditation #3—The Family White-Light Meditation

This meditation will purify and energize while building nonverbal family bonds. It can be done seated or lying down.

INSTRUCTIONS

"Close your eyes and let your body relax for a minute."

[Pause 5–10 seconds.]

"Now imagine a white light flowing into your feet. This soothing, pure white light relaxes and purifies wherever it goes, filling you with fresh, clean energy. . . . Now let the white light come up through your ankles . . . into your calves. Let your calves glow in the white light . . . then relax your knees and let the light come up into your thighs. Now your legs and feet are all glowing with pure white light. When you're ready, let the white light come up into your pelvis and stomach. Now, relax your chest and let your heart light up. Then let the white light come up through your throat and fill your face and mind with pure, soothing light. Picture your whole body bathed in white light from top to bottom."

[Pause 5–10 seconds.]

"Now expand your light until it bathes everyone around you."

[Pause 5–10 seconds.]

"Now allow all of our lights to become one light. One light, pure, unified, and strong."

[Pause 5–10 seconds.]

"Whenever you want to feel good, you can bathe yourself in the pure light to refresh and calm you."

[Pause.]

"Then when you are ready, you can slowly open your eyes and give yourself a good stretch."

Meditation #4—Golden Shower

This is a cleansing and purifying meditation that can leave you and the family feeling deeply refreshed. It makes use of our natural powers of imagination.

INSTRUCTIONS

"Close your eyes and imagine that as you relax and get comfortable, a soothing golden shower begins gently streaming down from above. This soothing, healthful shower streams over your head and flows down through your shoulders. As it flows down your head and shoulders, it cleanses you inside and out, clearing away all of the tension in your body. The golden shower flows down over your shoulders, taking away all of the tension in your shoulders, then flows down over your back and chest. As it streams down your back and flows down over your chest, it drains away any uncomfortable feelings you have stored down in your body. The soothing stream flows down over your stomach, letting all of the muscles relax completely. The golden shower flows down through your whole body, dissolving all the tension and making you feel clean, refreshed and calm. Take a moment to let the golden shower purify you completely, filling you with refreshing, clean energy."

[Pause 10 seconds.]

"Now imagine all of us bathed together in that golden shower. Picture the shower clearing away any uncomfortable feelings between us. Let us all be one inside that pure golden shower."

[Pause.]

"And then when you feel ready, slowly open your eyes and give yourself a big stretch."

Meditation #5—The Love Meditation

Love is the foundation of everything we hold dearest in families. This meditation gives us a way of being together for a few minutes to nurture that love and help it grow.

INSTRUCTIONS

"Down deep inside is a nice clear place that feels loving and kind. It's a place where you love yourself and other people. Sometimes we forget about how much love we have inside us and how much love there is around us all the time. Take a moment to close your eyes to let your mind get clear and your body relaxed."

[Pause 5–10 seconds.]

"Now let love grow inside you until you are deeply loving yourself. You can love yourself for all your feelings, all your thoughts, everything that's going on in you. Just let yourself fill up with love inside."

[Pause 5–10 seconds.]

"Now let that love expand to include everybody here. Just relax and let your love bathe them."

[Pause 5–10 seconds.]

"At the same time let their love bathe you, so that you feel completely loved right down to your toes."

[Pause 5 seconds.]

"Now let's fill the whole room up with love."

[Pause 5 seconds.]

"And when you are ready, let your eyes open."

FAMILY RELAXING
AND CENTERING ACTIVITIES

Relaxing and centering activities are good for growing families. If your family is growing, in all senses of the word, it can use activities that put all of you in touch with yourselves and each other. Relaxation and centering can give family members an inner sense of self that is as nutritious for our inner being as homemade bread is for our physical bodies.

Also, knowing how to relax and feel centered is a valuable skill that we can find uses for all our lives. A large number of illnesses are related to stress; anything we can learn to help us deal with stress will benefit us greatly in life. In addition, health is not only the absence of disease; it is actively *feeling good.* The following exercises actively promote a feeling of relaxed alertness that can assist us in whatever activities we do.

Activity #1—A Long, Deep
Relaxation Activity
for the Family

This activity will help the family explore the difference between tension and relaxation. It takes about 20 minutes and leads to a deep state of relaxation for most people. The process is done by lying down.

INSTRUCTIONS

"Lie back and let your body become as comfortable as it can. Wiggle around a little to explore the space you're in. Let your body make friends with the floor (or bed, etc.) that you are lying on. See if you can give up all resistance so that your body feels completely supported by the floor."

[Pause.]

"Now, as you relax, clench your right fist; clench Your fist tighter and tighter, and notice the tension as you do. Keep it clenched and feel the tension in your right fist, hand, and forearm. Now relax and let go. Let the fingers of your right hand become relaxed and note the contrast in your feelings. . . . Now, let yourself go and relax all over. . . . Again, clench your right fist really tight . . . hold it, and notice the tension again. . . . Now let go, relax; your fingers relax and you notice the difference once more. . . . Now repeat with your left fist. Clench your left fist while the rest of your body relaxes; clench that fist tighter . . . and now relax. Again note the contrast. . . . Repeat that again, clench the left fist, tight and tense . . . relax and feel the difference."

[Pause 10 seconds.]

"Now clench both fists tighter and tighter, forearms tense, fists tense . . . then relax; loosen your fingers and feel the soothing feeling of relaxation. Continue relaxing your hands and forearms more and more. . . . Now bend your elbows and tense your biceps, tense them more, and notice the tension. Then straighten out your arms, let them relax, and feel the difference again. Let the relaxing increase. . . . Again, tense your biceps; hold the tension. . . . Relax the arms and let go. Now relax your arms and let them feel completely supported. Let your arms feel comfortably heavy as you allow them to relax. . . . Continue relaxing your arms even further. Even when your arms seem fully relaxed, go even further into deeper and deeper feelings of relaxing.

"All of your muscles are feeling loose and heavy. Just be easy and comfortable. Wrinkle your forehead now; wrinkle it tightly. . . . Now stop wrinkling your forehead, relax, and smooth it out. The entire forehead and scalp become smoother as the relaxing increases. . . . Now frown and crease your brows. Let go again. Smooth out the forehead again. . . . Now, close your eyes tighter and tighter . . . feel the tension . . . then relax your eyes. Keep your eyes closed, peaceful, and easy (relaxed inside). Now clench your jaw; clench your teeth together; note the tension throughout the jaw. . . . Relax your jaw now. . . . Feel the relaxation all over your face, all over your forehead and scalp, eyes, jaws, lips, tongue, and throat. Now notice your neck muscles. Press your head back and feel the tension in your neck. Let your head return forward to a comfortable position, and note the feeling of relaxation. Shrug your shoulders. Push them up. Feel the tension in your shoulders and your back. . . . Let your shoulders relax. Let the relaxation spread deep into the shoulders, down into your back; relax your neck, your throat, your jaws, your face, as the deep relaxation grows deeper and deeper."

[Pause.]

"Relax your whole body deeply and peacefully. Feel the warm heaviness. Your breath comes freely in and out. As you breathe out just feel that relaxation. . . . Now relax your stomach. Tighten your stomach muscles; make your abdomen hard. Note the tension . . . then relax. Let the muscles relax and let the peaceful feelings come into your stomach. Again, press and tighten your stomach muscles. Hold the tension for a moment . . . then relax. Feel how relaxing your stomach helps you relax all over. Just let your stomach relax . . . deeper and deeper.

"Now tighten your buttocks, pelvis, and thighs. Relax and note the difference . . . tighten your muscles again. Tighter, tighter, then relax your pelvis, hips, and thighs. Now press your feet and toes downward so that your calf muscles can tense. . . . Note the tension. . . . Relax your calves and feet. . . . Keep relaxing for a moment. . . . Now let yourself relax all over. Relax your feet, ankles, calves, knees, thighs, buttocks, pelvis, and hips.

Now let the relaxation spread to your stomach and lower back. Relax more and more. Now let go in your upper back, chest, shoulders, and arms, all the way down to the tips of your fingers. Keep relaxing more and more. Let go of your neck and jaws and all of your face muscles. Let yourself relax deeply and fully.

"Now let yourself feel really relaxed by taking in a deep breath and slowly exhaling. Take in a long, deep breath and let it out very slowly. . . . Feel how peaceful and relaxed you can be."

[Pause.]

"Whenever you feel tense, or whenever you want to feel deeply relaxed, you can remember how this feels and slip back into this state. Now, we'll come back out, feeling rested and alert. I'll count down from 10 to 1, and when I hit 1, give yourself a big stretch and get up. 10–9–8–7–6–5–4–3–2–1."

Activity #2—Dissolving Family Tensions

This activity helps dissolve tension both inside our bodies and among one another. It is best done lying down.

INSTRUCTIONS

"Let your body relax as deeply as you can. . . . Move around until you find a spot where you can let the floor (or bed, couch, etc.) support you completely. Close your eyes and let them rest for a while."

[Pause.]

"Now tense your whole body for a moment as you take a deep breath. Hold the tension and hold your breath for a moment. . . . Now let go and exhale, letting your whole body relax. . . . Let go and relax even more. Your whole body can let go and feel really peaceful and comfortable."

[Pause 10 seconds.]

"Picture all of the tension in your head and face coming together into a big knot in your forehead. Study the knot for a moment; concentrate on it. . . . Now let it dissolve and melt, letting all the tension go from your head and face."

[Pause.]

"Now imagine all the tension in your throat coming together in a knot. In this knot are all the unspoken needs and feelings you have held back, all of the feelings you've swallowed. Put all of those tensions in the knot, then let it untie. . . . The knot melts and dissolves, taking all of the tension with it."

[Pause.]

"Now imagine all of the tension in your chest in a big knot around your heart. Feel how tense the knot is . . . then let the knot untie . . . melting and dissolving all the tension in your chest."

[Pause.]

"Now imagine all the tension in your stomach in a big knot down there. Feel it, see it, understand it. . . . Now let the knot untie . . . letting all your tension melt and dissolve."

[Pause.]

"Imagine that a big knot holds all of the rest of the tension in your body. Study the knot for a moment, feel it, understand it. . . . Now let it untie. . . . Let it melt and dissolve. . . . All of the tension drains from your body."

[Pause.]

"Now imagine that all your tensions between you and other people around you are a bunch of knots. Tensions build up around us, making knots between us and others. Feel and understand the knots. . . . Now let them untie, dissolving and melting all of the tension from between you. Then feel and enjoy the relaxation . . . no knots between you."

[Pause.]

"And when you are ready, slowly open your eyes, stretch, and get up feeling rested and alert."

Activity #3—Relaxing Away
Negative Feelings

This is a beautiful and powerful process that can solve problems at a deep level inside us and among us. It can be done seated or lying down.

INSTRUCTIONS

"Everybody has many different feelings during the day. Things may make us angry, scared, hurt, happy, or excited. Sometimes if you let yourself feel them at the time, they will dissolve and won't store up. But a lot of times we forget to let ourselves feel our feelings, so they get stored up inside us. Then they come out in ways that sometimes hurt us and people around us. We'll touch bases with a few different feelings that all of us feel. Take a moment to get your body as relaxed as you can. Close your eyes and let your mind relax."

[Pause 5–10 seconds.]

"Picture a thing or two that you may have felt angry about recently. . . . See it. . . . Feel it in your body. . . . Give yourself total permission to feel it . . . then relax and let it go."

[Pause 10 seconds.]

"Now picture a time or two when you've felt hurt . . . when your feelings have been hurt . . . or when you've felt rejected. . . . Just be with the feelings for a moment. . . . Let yourself feel them . . . then let them go and relax."

[Pause.]

"Let yourself get in touch with times you've felt scared recently. . . . Picture the situation in your

96

mind. . . . Feel it in your body. . . . Just let yourself
feel scared for a moment. . . . Then relax and let
the feelings go."

[Pause.]

"When you have feelings going on inside you,
take a moment to feel them deeply. This will keep
you from building them up and carrying them
around with you. Take a moment now to feel any
other feelings that we haven't touched."

[Pause.]

"Then when you are ready, bring yourself back to
alertness and give your body a good stretch."

Activity #4—Breathing Away Tension

This quick activity teaches a type of relaxation
that can be used later in any situation. You learn
it seated or lying down; you can use it even in
very active situations.

INSTRUCTIONS

"Now take a deep breath and hold it while tensing
every muscle in your body. Hold it . . . tighten . . .
now let it all go. . . . Exhale and relax."

[Pause.]

"Notice the feeling of your body relaxing and
settling down as your breath flows out. Take a

deep breath, hold it for a moment, then exhale and feel your body relax."

[Pause.]

"Again take a deep breath and tense all of your muscles . . . face, chest, stomach, legs . . . Hold it. . . . Now relax and exhale all your breath."

[Pause.]

"Now take a deep breath, hold it, and when you are ready, say 'relax' in your mind and let go, exhaling and relaxing. Feel your body relax on the exhale. Repeat several times."

[Pause.]

"Any time you want to relax, just take a deep breath, hold it for a moment, and then say 'relax' to yourself and exhale. At the same time you can feel your body relaxing and getting calmer. You can repeat it as often as you like."

[Pause.]

"Now take a moment to become relaxed and alert; then sit up and stretch."

Activity #5—The Centered Family

This activity can build a relaxed sense of personal centeredness while drawing the family closer together. It is best done seated in a circle.

INSTRUCTIONS

"Sit comfortably for a moment while your body
and mind settle down. Let your eyes close and
relax for a while."

[Pause.]

"Begin noticing the stream of air as you breathe
in through your nose. Feel it stream down through
your throat, your chest, down into your stomach.
Feel your breath peacefully and smoothly flowing
in and out of your body. Just focus on your
breathing for a moment."

[Pause.]

"And now find the spot down inside that is your
center. Some people feel it just beneath their
navel; others locate it elsewhere. As you breathe,
imagine the breath going right to your center. . . .
Feel yourself breathing with your center. Feel the
energy rushing in and out of your body through
your center."

[Pause 1–5 minutes.]

"Now as you breathe, expand your center out
from your body until you feel yourself connecting
with everyone else's centers here in the room."

[Pause 1 minute.]

"Now come back to your own center. You can become aware of your center anytime you want to feel more relaxed and confident. It's always there for you to feel. And now gradually let your awareness return to the room, and when you're ready, open your eyes and feel rested and alert."

Activity #6—Strengthening The Family Connection

Oftentimes when families come together, it is for mundane activities like eating or watching TV. Here, the family comes together to deepen their relationships with one another. Seated, in a circle, is the best arrangement for this activity.

INSTRUCTIONS

"Take a moment to let your body and mind relax. Close your eyes and begin focusing on your breath's coming in and out of your body."

[Pause 30 seconds.]

"Now imagine a golden light down in your center . . . a golden light that grows with each breath you take. It is relaxing and very powerful. Just notice it for a moment."

[Pause 10 seconds.]

"And now let that golden light expand until all our centers are connected in one light."

[Pause 15–30 seconds.]

"And now feel a golden light growing from your heart. Your heart and chest glow with the golden light."

[Pause 15 seconds.]

"And now let the golden light from your heart expand until it connects with all the other light. One light connects all hearts."

[Pause 15–30 seconds.]

"And now feel the golden light surrounding all of us. It connects all of us in its pure golden light."

[Pause as long as it feels good.]

"And now let the light rest in you, and when you are ready, bring your awareness back to the room and open your eyes, feeling calm and alert."

5

family
dreamwork

Our goal is to get closer to ourselves and one another to find out who we are, how we feel, and what we need. Anything we can do to move toward this goal will bring rich rewards. One tool that has been found very helpful in building closer families is dreams.* When family members talk about their dreams and work with them, they are dealing with a very deep level of human experience. To share a dream with another person is to reveal a secret treasure map to our souls. To explore these treasure maps together can be enlightening and fun. In addition, families who play with their dreams can learn many skills and abilities that can have a beneficial effect on their daily lives. Through dreamwork, it is possible to learn about your personality, uncover feelings and other issues that you are needing to deal with, and liberate more of your mind's potential.

We have talked earlier of how important it is to communicate about meaningful experiences in our lives. Dreams can be seen as some of the most meaningful

*I am grateful to Carol Leavenworth for her help in preparing this chapter.

experiences we have on a daily (or nightly) basis. Dreams are a direct print-out from the unconscious and are therefore free of the rules of the conscious mind, which is full of defenses, lies, beliefs, and other distortions. Also the dreams come to us in symbolic form, much as does a work of art like a painting, a mini-drama, or a film clip. Dreams, then, are made up of our deepest experiences, and they are creative works of art. To share dreams with others is to present them with the primal, creative parts of ourselves.

DREAM ACTIVITIES

Simply sharing dreams with family members is one of the best things that we can do. It is like sharing snapshots of ourselves with one another. I enjoy sharing dreams with my family at breakfast. Sometimes my daughter can hardly wait to tell me the latest in her dreamlife. Most often we do not *do* anything with a dream; it is simply shared and discussed in a playful, speculative way. Occasionally, however, one may want to go further with a dream. The activities that follow can be used to deepen our understanding of dreams and life.

Finding Out What Dreams Are Telling Us

Interpreting dreams is a creative challenge. Because their messages are often expressed symbolically, dreams are like puzzles waiting to be unraveled. Unfortunately, we have been led to believe that it takes an expert to interpret dreams correctly. Sometimes we hear that it may be dangerous to try to inerpret our own dreams. Actually, since your dreams are your own unique creations, no one can interpret your dreams as well as you can. By using a few simple techniques you can become an expert in interpreting your own dreams.

1. *Look for the overt message.* If you dream that your car has broken down, it is possible that you have failed to notice a strange noise or a slight difference in performance the last time you drove it. Often, when we are in a hurry or are preoccupied, our minds will note and store information to be brought out later. If these things do not occur to us during our waking hours, they may come up in a dream. This can also happen with things we know but have forgotten, such as appointments or special dates (like a friend's birthday).

2. *Uncover the hidden message in the dream story.* Dream stories are often entertaining fables or allegories about something in our lives. You can find the relationship of the dream story to waking life by telling or writing down the dream as if it were actually happening to you right now. Listen carefully as you relate the dream for similarities to experiences or thoughts you have had in the last day or so. The subject of the dream may become clear in the first two or three sentences. Then you can begin to explore what the dream is telling you about your feelings, wants, and needs by continuing to relate the dream in the present tense.

Ginny, a young married woman, dreamed that she was a courtier in medieval times. In her dreams she was trying to find the king to deliver an important message. This is what she wrote in her dream diary:

> I am walking down a dark road and I'm lost. I'm looking for the king but I can't find him. I have a pack on my back with a message in it. The pack is very heavy and I am tired of carrying it.

At this point, Ginny realized that her dream was about some things she wanted to discuss with her husband. She had been postponing their talk, waiting for an appropriate time. After analyzing the dream, Ginny could see that the emotional weight of this unfinished business was draining her. She decided to talk with her husband that night.

3. *Find the meaning of individual dream symbols.* The people or things in your dream may seem familiar or unfamiliar. They almost always represent something that is important in your life right now. You can find their meaning by using your creative imagination to "become" that person or thing for a moment and, as the dream symbol, tell your story.

Ann, a career woman who participated in a weekly therapy group, had a dream that took place under a large tree. To find the meaning of the tree symbol, Ann closed her eyes and said, "I am the oak tree in Ann's dream." Then, as the oak tree, she went on to relate all the thoughts that come to mind about the tree's qualities, feelings, and wants and its purpose in her dream. Ann found that the tree symbolized tradition and stability. The image related to a choice she was trying to make between two houses she and her family were considering purchasing.

By giving her symbol a voice, she was able to find out some important things about her priorities.

It is possible to have a dialogue with your dream symbols by first allowing the symbol to speak and then, as yourself, asking any questions that come to mind. As soon as a question is posed, you can use your imagination to become the symbol again and relate the first thoughts that come to mind. You can also allow your dream symbols to speak to one another in this way. Just say what pops into your head no matter how silly or trivial the response may seem. It is helpful to use a tape recorder or ask a friend to make notes as you do this so that your mind is free and open.

Another method for understanding dream symbols is based on the theory that every part of a dream represents a part of the dreamer. Just as Ann's oak tree symbolized her feelings about tradition, any dream symbol may represent a belief, quality, feelings, or value of ours that is asking to be acknowledged. Conflict in dreams may be our attempt to bring various parts of ourselves into agreement.

Let's say that you had a dream with several components: a car, a tree, a horse, and a boat. To discover what part of yourself a symbol may represent, you can again become that symbol in your imagination and say, "The car is the part of me that . . . " "The tree is the part of me that . . ." By completing this sentence several times, you will have a good idea what aspects of yourself are expressing themselves through the symbol.

4. *Identify the feelings under the dream.* Most vivid dreams get their energy from strong feelings we have had. A nightmare's intensity comes from very strong

feelings seeking expression. Most other dreams are also expressing feelings that we may not have noticed or given enough attention to during the day. Most of us have more than one feeling about everything in our lives. We may love a child and also be angry with him or her. We may be happy about being chosen to hold an important position while still feeling uneasy about assuming the responsibility. In working life we may concentrate on some of the feelings we are having and ignore the others. When this happens, we often will have a dream to remind us that our other feelings are just as real and important.

You can discover the dream's feelings by returning to the dream in your imagination and re-experiencing it as fully as possible. Notice how your body responds to what is happening in the dream and how these feelings are like feelings you have had in your waking life. Stay with the feelings for a moment and experience them as deeply as you can. If you remember to acknowledge them in the future, they will probably not come back in your dreams.

Many more dream activities can be found in *The Centering Book* and *The Second Centering Book*, and if you find dreamwork particularly fascinating, the bibliography in the latter book will provide a treasure map for other sources.

Because most dreams have more than one meaning, you may want to use two or more techniques to understand each dream. The best way to choose a technique is to follow your intuition. Use the technique that you think you will enjoy or that seems to be the most profitable. If one method is not satisfying, you can always try another. You can also alternate techniques from time to time to get a feeling for the kind of information each one will yield. Dream interpretation can be most beneficial when done in a spirit of play and exploration. By interpreting some of the dreams that arise spontaneously, you may find new solutions to problems that confront you and learn more about your inner self.

HOW TO PUT YOUR DREAMS TO WORK FOR YOU

Once you have gained some skills in dream interpretation, you can begin to use your dreams more actively to help you in many ways. The following case histories show how two people used their dreams to assist them in solving real-life problems.

Jane was feeling especially tired and irritable. For months she had been eagerly anticipating these last few weeks before her twins started school and she returned to the career she had begun before they were born. Now her energy and good humor seemed to be deserting her just when she needed them most.

After failing to pinpoint the reason for her discomfort, Jane decided to ask her dreams for help. Just before falling asleep, she gave herself the suggestion that her dreams would tell her why she felt so tired. Early the next morning she awoke feeling very sad. She remembered dreaming that she had been searching vainly for the family photo album containing pictures of the twins from babyhood through their toddler years. It did not take Jane long to realize what her dream was telling her. She had been ignoring her sad feelings about leaving an important stage in her life. Once Jane was able to recognize both her sadness and her excitement about the coming changes in her life, her energy began to return. As she began to make a point of acknowledging all her feelings to herself, her husband, and her children, she felt calmer. By sharing more of herself with those close to her, her relationships entered a new stage of warmth and closeness.

Mary had been trying for weeks to decide whether or not to take a week-long trip to a distant city to attend an ecology conference. Although her husband and children assured her that they would be fine, Mary felt uneasy about leaving them and about the expense involved. Finally, she decided to consult her dreams. Before falling asleep, she said to herself, "I want to know if I should attend the conference. I want a dream that will tell me 'yes' or 'no.' "

That night Mary dreamed she was walking through a beautiful wilderness meadow. She was drawn to a grove of trees. As she approached, she became aware that there was something strange about one of the trees. In fact, it was not a tree at all, but a traffic light shining a steady green. On the basis of her dream and her family's urging, Mary attended the conference, where she met a representative from a statewide energy-consulting association. Eventually this contact led to a part-time research position with the firm.

Anyone can use dreams to learn new things and answer difficult questions just as Jane and Mary did.

Since our dreams are nothing but statements—symbolic or straightforward—about our experiences, we will dream about those things that are in the forefront of our experience. Programing our dreams to help us with specific concerns involves both clearing the decks mentally and physically of other issues and bringing vividly to mind our problem or question as we are about to fall asleep. The following steps will help you program your dreams in any way you wish.

1. *Create a positive sleep environment.* If you can make your sleeping place as comfortable and pleasant as possible, you will remove distractions that may occupy your dreaming mind. Noise, too much heat or cold, or an uncomfortable bed may interfere with your dream program. Even though you are asleep, the awareness of a hated painting over your head can invade your dream world.

2. *Clear your body.* Indigestion, muscle tension, or drugs taken at bedtime can disturb dream patterns. Eating lightly or not at all before bedtime and avoiding alcohol in the evening will enhance your ability to dream creatively. If your body feels tense, you can take a few minutes to relax your muscles from head to toe in order to facilitate deeper rest and more productive dreams.

3. *Clear your mind.* Worries about unfinished chores can fill our dream life with the dire consequences of leaving tasks undone. Similarly, thoughts about the pressures of the coming day may creep into our dreams if we do not release our concerns prior to sleep. As much as possible, finish tasks begun before sleep. You can make a schedule of activities for the coming day and rest more easily knowing you will not forget an important responsibility. Some things cannot be resolved in a few minutes. Deciding when you will handle them and making a firm commitment with yourself to do so can help to remove these concerns from your dream life.

4. *Clear your feelings.* As we have seen, feelings left over from the day can come up in dreams. By spending a few minutes just before sleep in reviewing the day and allowing yourself to experience agan any feelings of anger, sadness, fear, and joy, you can prepare emotionally for more creative dreaming.

CONCLUSION

Family dreamwork can be a tool for your family to grow closer by sharing meaningful experiences. Along the way they may also learn some important ideas about living by learning to listen to their dreams. Often people who learn to work with their dreams find that the answers they have been seeking about themselves and the world are as close as their pillow.

discussions

CHILD DEVELOPMENTAL STAGES AND WHAT TO DO ABOUT THEM

Question: What are the main stages of child development, and what do we do about them?

Answer: There are different versions depending on which theorist you talk to, but from a very practical standpoint, here are some observations you can use for guidelines.

For the first six months of life, the issues are basically trust and answering the question "Can I get my needs met here?" If the nurturing contact is there, usually, of course, with mother, most of the child's questions about whether or not she can trust and whether or not he can get his needs met are resolved.* If the contact is not a satisfying one from the child's point of view, then she carries forward into the next stage judgments that the world is an unsafe place and a place of scarcity and want.

*I'll use "he" and "she" alternately in this discussion.

117

In general, we can consider that the unresolved issues in each stage will be carried forward to the next stage and put "on hold" for later resolution. Obviously many of our very young issues get carried forward into adult life. Most of us, under stress, revert to the type of behavior seen in the stage of development we are stuck on. Thus, one adult may act like the popular conception of a two-year-old, another may feel untrustful, and another may cry a lot. The ability to spot these patterns and deal with them is, in my opinion, one of the marks of an enlightened adult.

The main needs in the 0–6-months stage are for the basics: food, warmth, strokes, air. About six months of age, the baby moves on into a more exploratory stage. A major need is to satisfy hunger for stimulation and exploration. Parents can respond by making the environment safe for exploration, by providing lots of stimulation, and by allowing a bit more independence. Parents at this stage, particularly mother if she does the majority of parenting, must monitor their own energy levels. The parenting of a child in the exploratory stage is a most energy-consuming affair; if parents do not factor this in and respond by structuring lots of rest time, burn-out can occur.

If children during this period are not encouraged to explore, or if their explorations bring mainly negative consequences, the child may leave this period with a fear of exploring the unknown, which can hamper creativity later in life.

At around 18 months of age, children begin to separate from mother and enter a period of autonomy and learning to think for themselves. It is a complicated period in which the child must master several tricky issues. One, she must learn that she can be on her own, think for herself, and still get the love she needs. Parents will still love her if she is out of sight. Then, to complicate matters further, toilet training generally occurs here, and the child must learn how to relate to authority. When we do not learn to relate to authority effectively, we often either rebel (the "you can't make me" stance that parents of two-year-olds are very familiar with) or we overadapt. The latter posture is a decision that says, "Okay, I'll do it your way but you'll never know how I really feel inside." Both of these ways cause many problems later in life.

If parents are unwilling to let the child be separate, then a dependency is fostered that can hamper the child's later ability to be autonomous in life. This can be spotted in adult life if we are fearful of being on our own, have to let others think for us, and flip-flop back and forth between asserting our independence through rebellion and then feeling dependent again.

From two-and-a-half years old to school age, children find out about the society they are in. They find out what it means to be a woman, what it means to be a man, and other aspects of socialization. Here they find out if they are comfortable being who they are, if they can handle the feelings inside them, and if who they are on the outside works in their family and society. Sexual feelings awaken for the first time in this age group, then wane until puberty.

When children go to school, they enter the period of what Freud called latency, because he observed that the sexual drive went underground and was latent during this phase. The term is still used by some theorists, although it is not descriptive of the actions children engage in during this stage. It would be more descriptive to think of this stage as one of competence building or finding out how the world works. This is also a stage in which the child must learn to separate reality from fantasy and build a workable model of reality. That is why this stage is full of arguing, hassling about rules, and asking "Why?" How else would we build a model of reality? Although arguing is not pleasant to hear, it is one of the few ways we have of testing one model of reality against another. The important thing to remember about arguing is that *what* the argument is about is largely irrelevant. It is the process of arguing that gets the job done. If we understand this latter point, we may take the process a little less seriously, thus having some sanity left over for the teenage years when we will seriously need it.

The teenage years begin with a mad confusion of bodily sensations awakening inside. The teenager must learn how to relate to sexual feelings in addition to the other feelings; also he must gain a workable form of independence and learn to relate to authority. There is also the awesome task of learning to be with the peer group, both male and female. Can we be real, or must we put on a mask? How can I be on my own although I'm still somewhat dependent on parents? How can I control my feelings and act appropriately? One parent of three teenagers said that it was like living with three miniature manic-depressives.

Teenagers have a second chance to rework the unresolved issues from earlier stages. They have an opportunity to form trusting relationships, learn how to relate to authority, learn how to be on their own in a responsible way, deal with their feelings, and make it socially. It is obvious that we carry many of these same issues into adult life, leading one psychologist to describe adult life as one long attempt to resolve adolescence.

In child and adult development, it does little good to decry our unresolved issues. A more enlightened attitude is to acknowledge that this is the way things are, then go about the business of spotting and dissolving our limitations and those of others in a loving and straightforward way.*

HOW TO GIVE PERMISSIONS
WITHOUT BEING PERMISSIVE

Responsible and thoughtful parents give children (and one another) rich and frequent permissions. Permissions are enabling statements, both verbal and nonverbal, that help free up more of children's potential. Many permissions have to do with feelings.

> It is okay to feel.
> It is okay to feel scared
> > hurt
> > angry
> > joyful.
>
> Sexual feelings are normal and natural.
> All your feelings are all right.
> *And,* here are some healthy ways to express your various feelings.

*The recently developing field of adult developmental stages is described in Gail Sheehy's popular book *Passages,* as well as in Roger Gould's *Transformations* and Daniel Levinson's *The Seasons of a Man's Life.*

Other permissions are to help people see that they can think and solve problems, be successful, be themselves, and be creative, loveable, and compassionate. By giving people permission to be intuitive and even psychic, these aspects of us, now considered special, may in time become regarded as natural.

Giving permissions has nothing to do with permissiveness. Permissiveness is a failure to set and keep limits. Permissions involve communicating what you like to see in people and enabling them to open up new vistas for themselves. Permissions is an antidote for permissiveness. For example, you may say to a seven-year-old boy, "It's okay for you to have fun and feel good, and I want you to stay with me and not run around the store." This type of statement lets the person know that his feelings are fine, but there are some actions that are going to work better with you than with others. Permissiveness is when limits are not set until the behavior becomes intolerable. Permissiveness is lazy parenting; giving permissions is vigilant and caring parenting.

===

A Family Therapist Discusses Anger and How to Deal With It

By Gary A. Cosel,
Psychologist

[From my own experience I have found anger to be a difficult feeling to deal with. There is an art to learning

how to express anger in ways that are not hurtful to
ourselves and others. I asked an associate of mine, Gary
Cosel, to discuss anger in more detail. —G.H.]

Most of us are beginning to realize the importance
of acknowledging, feeling, and expressing our emotions.
We are realizing that unfelt feelings refuse to remain
buried and will come back to haunt us in the form of
annoying thoughts, physical tension or illness, and
similar recurring conflicts. A recent case will illustrate.
Nancy, a patient, was subjected to rejecting parents.
As a young child she was left unattended when she
experienced nightmares and other natural fears of
injury, death, and abandonment. Somewhere in Nancy's
development she acquired the message from her parents
that it was unacceptable to feel scared. If Nancy
communicated her deepest fears to her parents, Nancy's
mother would panic and either change the subject or
express, "Don't you know how much it hurts Mom to
hear you speak that way? I've got enough problems of
my own; I can't worry about yours." Later, if confronted
with fearful situations in adulthood, Nancy would resist
the feelings. She would entertain thoughts such as "If
I'm scared or begin to cry I might lose control and go
crazy." Another thought was, "People won't like me if I
express my feelings." Nancy buried her feelings and
began experiencing symptoms of chronic constipation,
diarrhea, and burning between the shoulder blades. Her
fears increased until culminating in a claustrophobic
condition.

Expressing feelings can have a refreshing effect.
Those people who have received messages from parents
to feel their emotions experience the cleansing relief

from a powerful cry. Others also understand the benefits of sharing sadness and fear with close friends and family.

Anger is an emotion that continues to confuse and threaten us. We have not yet acknowledged anger as an acceptable feeling, nor have we learned how to express and receive anger. We are often appalled by our children's raising their voices at us; we may experience our shoulders tensing in anger at the thought of a child's being disrespectful to an adult by expressing anger. We have spanked children, washed their mouths out with soap, and revoked special privileges for their expressions of anger. Later, in adult life, we may feel guilty after getting angry. This is the legacy from the punishment we received when we expressed our anger in childhood. .

The purpose of this discussion is to propose a new outlook on anger. We will look at anger as a necessary emotional expression and illustrate how some of our current outlets for anger are nontherapeutic and unhealthy. We will also see the importance of teaching parents and children lifelong skills for expressing anger in direct and appropriate ways. In addition, we will look at ways for adults to receive anger without being threatened.

ANGER: A NECESSARY EMOTIONAL EXPERIENCE

Much of our religious tradition has given us repressive and often confusing messages about anger. We are warned to "turn the other cheek" and deny our feelings instead of giving ourselves permission to feel anger deeply. As mortals we realize how impossible the injunction against anger can be. As a matter of fact, it seems the more we attempt to deny, resist, or bury our anger toward others, the greater is the intensity and frequency of this emotion. For example, a friend of mine, Robert, had an employer who had repeatedly required him to work long hours for a minimal salary. He had been awaiting that yearly evaluation, which would surely propel him to an administrative position. When no such advancement occurred, Robert felt hurt and angry but would not admit this to himself. He had always maintained the belief that people would think of him as too emotional to be competent if the real feelings emerged. Robert began frequenting the local bar in an attempt to drown his emotions. His wife became the indirect target for his bottled anger when he began to withdraw from her and frequently blame her for overcooked meals, mismanagement of the children, etc.

WHAT MAKES US "STUFF" ANGER?

Contrary to belief, anger is as natural and normal an emotion as any other. The threat of anger evolves from confusing anger with aggressive behavior or hostile motivations. Anger is nothing more than the physiological arousal of increased adrenalin flow and the attendant muscular constriction of shoulders, neck, arms, and stomach. It is the fear of misdirected behavior resulting from the physiological arousal, which guides us to "stuff the feelings." If Robert had been taught early in childhood to honor his anger and to release it in appropriate ways, the painful behavior toward his wife could have been avoided.

Parents who refuse to allow their children to express anger, and those who do not teach their children appropriate releases, will find the anger coming out in the form of misdirected behavior. As stated earlier, anger is a natural emotion that everyone experiences. It will emerge in some form. Misdirected behavior resulting from anger takes many shapes. The acting-out child includes the school bully who provokes fights and steals from other students; this is the teacher's nightmare. He cheats on exams, runs around the room, and is belligerent to teachers' demands. Misdirected behavior resulting from anger may also take a passive–aggressive form. This is the child who passively resists adult requests by refusing to do classwork, failing assignments, not talking, or saying, "I can't do it." Both the acting-out and passive-aggressive forms of anger are clear expressions of "I'm angry and I'm going to let you know by making your life miserable." These children are indirectly asking for a battle so that they can vent their anger.

Fear may also be a form of mismanaged anger. Children who acquire the message from parents that anger is dangerous may "stuff" their anger in all situations that normally call for it. For example, Daniel, a patient who is being verbally abused by other elementary-school children, resists the anger and experiences intense fear. Because he has not defended himself with an angry posture, he becomes the victim of further attacks. Daniel may begin perceiving the world

as an overpowering place in which he needs to defend
himself against probable injustices. The arousal of
chronic fear may lead to thoughts of inferiority and
lack of power.

When an individual has acknowledged and
expressed the anger appropriately, he is in a healthier
frame of mind to effect positive problem solving.
Children are more available to look at the dynamics of
how the problem emerged and how to avoid it in the
future. Many times during crises parents demand that
their children understand the situation and arrive at a
new plan of behavior without first allowing an emotional
release. No doubt parents are justified in expecting
children to realize why and how they got angry, but
only following the appropriate release. Without this
permission, parents might note the difficulty that the
child experiences.

CURRENT OUTLETS FOR ANGER:
NONTHERAPEUTIC AND UNHEALTHY

Parents who understand the effectiveness of allowing
their children to express anger often comment, "We
know that Michael needs to burn off some tension, so
we've enrolled him in a sports camp. There he can learn
the fundamentals of boxing, football, and jogging. Don't
you think sports are the finest outlet for releasing
anger?" To Michael's parents' surprise, and I'm sure to
others', this needs to be answered with a no. For
example, running, basketball, tennis, and other sports

are all activities that fatigue the body and temporarily reduce tension. However, participants do not become aware of feelings, the issues that provoked the emotional tension, or the ways to resolve problems. Proponents of dealing with anger through sports ignore the circumstances that provoked the feelings. They may continue to exercise away the stress without uncovering and dealing with the reasons for it.

HOW CAN WE DETERMINE WHETHER OUR CHILDREN EXPRESS ANGER APPROPRIATELY?

Let's refer again to our three personalities resulting from mismanaged anger—acting-out, passive-aggressive, and fearful. Here is a short inventory on our beliefs and practices concerning the expression of anger.

1. Do I allow my child to express anger?

   Yes _____   No _____

2. If not, how does my child receive that message?
   Examples: Parents verbally reprimand the child for anger.

   Child never sees parents argue.

   Child watches as parents' verbal battles lead to divorce.

   _____

   _____

3. How is my child allowed to release anger?
   Examples: Screaming at parents anywhere, including
   public places.

   Fighting with siblings.

   Damaging others' property.

   Talking back to teachers.

   _____

   _____

4. List five ways to express anger that you feel would
   be appropriate.
   Example: Directly stating "I'm angry."

   _____

   _____

   _____

   _____

   _____

5. List five ways that you would not like to see your
   child express anger.
   Examples: all the ways listed under #3.

   _____

   _____

   _____

   _____

   _____

After working with many families, I have evolved some criteria for expressions of anger. The anger release is appropriate if it does not:

1. Endanger self or others.
2. Damage property.
3. Embarrass or threaten someone in a public setting.
4. Involve passive–aggressive or acting-out behaviors.

Expressions of anger are effective when they have minimal negative consequences. Destructive contact sports and/or fighting with friends, siblings, and others may be dangerous. Throwing, kicking, and damaging property regardless of who owns it is costly. Slamming bedroom doors or racing the family car is not only endangering others but may damage valuable property.

Passive–aggressive and acting-out expressions of anger are misdirected behaviors. These behaviors alienate significant adults, frequently causing parents to become angry and retaliate with punishment. Families with children manifesting these chronic patterns would benefit from psychological services.

Embarrassing or verbally threatening someone in a public setting may also create a disturbance. Ideal as it may seem to express verbal anger at anyone in any place, society has established some rules for appropriate behavior. One standard is that people should withhold the expression of angry behavior when in the presence of authority figures. It is not in children's best interests to express anger toward parents, teachers, employers, judges, and policemen unless given permission in a private setting to do so. Parents need to instruct their children how to "stuff" the feelings at times and allow them safe release when back in the privacy of the home.

WHAT ARE APPROPRIATE
ANGER RELEASES?

The signficant message I am attempting to convey through this discussion is that *feeling angry is a natural emotion. Parents can give their children total permission to experience the sensations of anger.* Allowing children to feel anger without necessarily acting it out may alone be effective for the child to work through a conflict.

In my psychotherapeutic practice I have identified four avenues by which children can, when needed, appropriately express anger. One rational technique is to make an "assertive statement." An assertive statement is built on the premise that both people involved in the conflict acknowledge the other's rights to his or her wants. Each person rationally states his or her feelings, telling what disturbed him or her about the other's behavior and stating what he or she wants. A plan is devised so that both individuals are heard and both get what they want.

For example, nine-year-old Michelle, who had recently learned communication skills in school, is angry at Dad because he doesn't play with her when he arrives home from work. Michelle calmly states her feelings—"I'm disappointed and angry at you, Dad"— then the reasons and what she wants—"You seem to avoid me when you come home from work. I want you to play with me." Dad has no reason to be offended since Michelle has not attacked him. He states his sorrow to hear Michelle's disappointment and shares, "You want to play with me when I get home, but I don't feel like playing right away because I'm so tired from working at the office." Dad then suggests that they think of solutions that will please both of them. In a few minutes, they arrive at a solution that both of them accept. Dad promises to play with Michelle, provided she waits until he has finished with dinner. He will have his rest period, after which Michelle will get her play period. This "no lose" assertive statement can only be effective if the adult recipient will communicate at an equal level. The child armed with this communication style might experiment with significant people and come to his or her own conclusions as to who will listen and respond with respect. Parents are not always available to provide information to the child as to whether the adult in authority will be receptive. Parents can provide reassurance for those unsuccessful attempts.

The second form of appropriate angry expressions are what I call "psychophysical releases." These appropriate aggressive techniques are effectively used in my psychotherapeutic practice with children. Parents can also use these exercises in the home with success. However, I would recommend that parents evaluate their values and attitudes toward this process before implementing it in the home. The parents' commitment to following through consistently without becoming emotionally threatened is a prerequisite to the success of these exercises. I recommend that these techniques be practiced within a room of the home that is designated by the parents as the "Angry Room."

Limiting this release to a private, safe area establishes clear rules that this type of aggressive expression anywhere else is inappropriate. Psychophysical releases are expressions that integrate body movement, emotional response, and mental imagery. For example, Joshua, a young patient, became furious at his sister for breaking his favorite toy. Joshua's mother was quick to notice a potential for aggressive behavior. She lead him into the Angry Room, where he was given permission to pound a tennis racquet against pillows (body movement). She provided Joshua with the suggestion that he could yell and feel angry (emotional response) while imagining all the things he felt angry about (mental imagery).

Following the psychophysical release, parents can emphasize more adaptive responses by asking Joshua to make an assertive statement to his sister, telling her his feelings and what he wants. In some situations the assertive statement cannot be made because the anger was directed toward someone in an unreceptive authority position or toward someone far removed from the Angry Room. In this case, the parents can act as the substitute recipient for the child's assertive statement. For example, Andrew, another young patient, comes home from school angry at his teacher for wrongfully disciplining him for another child's misbehavior. Andrew realizes that he has to "stuff" the feelings at school or receive further punishment from his teacher. Following the psychophysical release in the Angry Room, he is in a rational posture to inform a parent what his feelings were, reasons for the arousal, and what he wants, and even brainstorm a plan for getting it.

Psychophysical releases in the Angry Room are

practiced during crises when the person is far too angry to behave rationally and make an assertive statement. An emotional expression is necessary before the individual can calmly determine how he or she became angry and what he or she wants. As in Andrew's case, psychophysical releases can be vented in the Angry Room when the child must "stuff" the feelings because of an unreceptive authority figure.

Psychophysical releases in the Angry Room can also be practiced when there are no crises. An individual experiencing tension can visit the Angry Room to relieve stress and gain insight as to the source of the irritability. Psychophysical releases can be exercised daily by children to fantasize their sense of power over the natural fears of monsters, animals, and ghosts. This practice will reduce nightmares and excessive fears.

The following is a menu of some aggressive psychophysical releases that have proved successful in my work with children. Parents can choose the exercises according to their interests and values. Although the focus here is on children's anger, parents are also encouraged to make use of the Angry Room and the following activities.

MENU OF TECHNIQUES

Activities to do by oneself in the Angry Room:

1. *Using a Tennis Racquet to Hit a Couch or Bed.* Stand with feet shoulder-width apart, knees slightly bent, at arms' length from the couch, with two hands on the racquet. Bring the racquet back over the head (as opposed to over the left or right shoulder) and slam the

face of the racquet against the seat of the couch. A loud sound will be made upon impact. Repeat this at the speed and length of time desired. The individual can imagine the couch representing any person or situation, and is requested to make a vocal expression (e.g., scream, yell "no," make animal sounds).

2. *Pounding Cushions or Punching Bag with Fists.* Use similar visual imagination and vocal expression, as in 1.

3. *Kicking Cushions.* Lie flat on your back with a cushion propped against the wall. Kick against the cushion with the bottoms of the feet. Lie flat on your back with a cushion resting on the floor. Kick cushion with the heels of your feet. Stand upright with the cushion on the floor. Have a child jump repeatedly on the cushion.
Use similar visual imagination and vocal expression for each exercise as in 1.

4. *Jumping Up and Down and Throwing a Temper Tantrum.* Use similar visual imagination and vocal expression.

5. *Knocking Blocks.* Children can build tall structures out of durable blocks and knock them down. They can imagine that the disliked person is inside the building.

Activities to do in the Angry Room with parent, sibling, or friend not associated with any present crises*:

---

*Aggression against a parent involved in the conflict may create guilt for the child. Aggression against a friend or sibling involved in the conflict reinforces inappropriate expressions of anger.

6. *Pillow Battles.* The child is allowed to imagine the other person as the situation, animal, monster, ghost, or person toward which the anger is directed. Vocal expression is encouraged. The child in need of the release should be allowed to dominate the battle.

7. *Fighting with Inflated Paper Sacks.* This is a safe battle with two large inflated grocery sacks. Again, allow the child to imagine the other as the object of anger, encourage vocal expression. The child should be allowed to dominate the battle.

8. *Newspaper Battle.* Save all newspapers for one week. Give half to each participant. The goal is to imagine the other as the object of anger. Crumple pieces of newspaper and throw it at the other. By the end of the battle the participants will be knee-deep in newspaper.

9. *Water-Gun Battle.* The object is to drench your partner.

The third form of anger release is through imagery. This is a meditative process (as opposed to the active behavioral approaches already introduced). Imagery* is the simple process of closing your eyes and imagining angry scenes. Some examples include: throwing bricks through plate-glass windows, hitting an automobile with a sledge hammer, or any imagined aggressive scene the individual chooses. If we can *consciously* use aggressive imagery, it can keep us from unconsciously fantasizing about our anger.

This release can be exercised when the assertive statement and Angry Room cannot be used. The person

---

In The Mind's Eye, by Arnold Lazarus, Ph.D. (New York: Rawson Associates Publishers, Inc., 1977).

merely finds a quiet area and lets the visual images appear. A few minutes is usually sufficient to provide relief. Additional psychophysical releases and assertive statements can later be exercised to dissolve the conflict entirely. Again, a clear distinction is drawn between fantasy and reality. The person is reminded that imagining aggressive actions toward others is permissible, but acting them out is inappropirate.

A fourth strategy for anger relase is simply to be aware of the anger inside until it dies away. With anger, take a few deep breaths and imagine letting yourself feel the anger in every cell of your body. This is a sophisticated process that usually requires some practice before being effective. Once mastered, it can be used anywhere with any feeling.

HOW PARENTS CAN DEAL
WITH THE THREAT
OF CHILDREN'S ANGER

There will be situations in which the child loses control and begins aiming anger at an adult. Some willing adults can deal effectively with this conflict by making assertive statements or directing the child to the Angry Room without losing their own patience. The parent realizes that rage is an unacceptable behavior unless confined to a private place so that others will not be disturbed. This parent may choose to remain in the Angry Room to only listen to the child's rage or may choose to leave the child alone until he or she is settled.

If the adult remains in the Angry Room, the only rule I propose is not to engage the child in any verbal or physical battle. Give the child permission to vent a psychophysical expression by him- or herself, or listen to his verbal rage without comment.

There are coping strategies parents can use if they find themselves emotionally threatened by the child's anger. They should first determine their core feelings and beliefs. Parents who have guilty feelings might believe that it is their fault that the child is angry.

Parents who respond with anger might look deeper to determine whether the anger is a facade for deeper feelings of fear. Many times we hide our fears by reacting with anger. Typical beliefs creating fear are

Fear of abandonment—My child might leave home.

Fear of losing love or care—My child won't love me anymore.

Fear of helplessness—My child might lose control of his emotions. The anger will get him into trouble.

Parents can find relief by simply acknowledging, "I'm scared" and sharing their fears directly with children. It is normal to be scared of intense emotion. By dealing directly with their feelings and those of their children, parents may begin to feel the heavy burdens of anger, fear, and guilt lift from their own shoulders.

[Anger is a feeling that troubles many of us. We all need as many skills as we can get to deal with anger effectively. For other approaches to dealing with children's anger

and our own, see Tom Gordon's Parent Effectiveness Training, *Babcock and Keepers'* Raising Kids OK, *and* How to Love Every Minute of Your Life *by me and Carol Leavenworth. Each book sheds light from a different angle on the different problems of anger.—G.H.*]

A LAZY PERSON'S GUIDE TO EFFECTIVE DISCIPLINE

Because I am lazy and like to spend more time enjoying kids than hassling with them about rules and discipline problems, I have evolved some general ideas on how to set things up so that a minimum of time is spent worrying about discipline. It takes an hour or two of forethought to set up the kind of system I am describing, but it will save you much time later. It is a common-sense system that I have used with my own offspring, with families in counseling, and with other groups with whom I have consulted.

The basic idea is to set things up so that the positive behavior of children pays off for them. As a parent, you arrange it so that kids do what you want, and then they can do what they want. For example,

Eat your vegetables, and then you can have dessert.

Clean up your room then you can go out and play.

Do your homework before you watch TV.

Finish your chores, and then you can have the car.

Although this may sound ridiculously simple, you might be surprised at the number of families in which these kinds of agreements are reversed. If this is the case, then Mom, for example, has to drag Son away from the TV set to do homework. If the agreements are spelled out neatly beforehand and consistently maintained, many arguments and power struggles can be avoided.

If rules like these are set up, it helps teach children a valuable lesson about how the world works. In general, the privileges in the world are available to those who fulfill their responsibilities.

FACTS ABOUT FEELINGS

Here is some basic information on feelings that, if we can learn it early in life, can save us much energy later on.

1. *All feelings are all right.* All our feelings are okay. It's what we do with them that determines whether or not we get into trouble with ourselves and one another. Too often we communicate to people that the feeling itself is wrong. This type of disapproval only drives feelings deeper and makes them harder to deal with later. Our best bet is to let people know that it's okay for them to feel all their feelings, but that there are ways of expressing them that seem to work better than others.

2. *If we deny or ignore feelings, they will sneak back when we are not looking.* Feelings that we do not

pay attention to return in many different forms. They provide the fuel for bad dreams and irritating daytime thoughts. They also cause problem behavior. For example, some anger that is buried in the morning may come back that evening in the form of a sarcastic remark. Much of the tension that we feel in our bodies is due to trying to deal with feelings by tightening up on them.

3. *Things go smoother when we accept our basic feelings and then look for straightforward ways of expressing them.* Some of our basic feelings are fear, anger, sadness, excitement, and joy. If we let ourselves feel those, we are resonating with a deep part of us.

In expressing feelings, honesty and straightforwardness work best. If you're angry, say, "I'm angry." If your're scared, say "I'm scared." It sounds easy, but it takes much practice to master the art of doing it "under fire."

4. *If you don't like some feeling you are feeling, love it to death.* We are much too hard on ourselves for our feelings. The critical approach is usually not very useful. It does not make the feeling go away permanently, and it makes us feel bad about ourselves. The best way we have found to eliminate an unwanted feeling is to love and understand it.

index